Sharon Maxwell Magnus is an award-winning writer. Her awards include the Catherine Packenham Award for Women Journalists and the Industrial Society Media Award for articles on women in the workplace. She has worked for a number of magazines including *Cosmopolitan* and *She*, as well as a wide variety of national newspapers. Sharon has written three other books, including *Making Serious Money At Home*. She is not a millionaire, but is working on it.

think yourself rich

how to develop the
MIND OF A MILLIONAIRE

Sharon Maxwell Magnus

Vermilion
LONDON

5 7 9 10 8 6 4

Copyright © Optomen Television 2003

Optomen Television has asserted its moral right to be identified as the author of this work in accordance with the Copyright, Design and Patents Act 1988.

First published in the United Kingdom in 2003
by Vermilion, an imprint of Ebury Press
Random House UK Ltd.
Random House
20 Vauxhall Bridge Road
London SW1V 2SA

Random House Australia (Pty) Limited
20 Alfred Street, Milsons Point, Sydney,
New South Wales 2061, Australia

Random House New Zealand Limited
18 Poland Road, Glenfield,
Auckland 10, New Zealand

Random House (Pty) Limited
Endulini, 5A Jubilee Road, Parktown 2193, South Africa

Random House UK Limited Reg. No. 954009
www.randomhouse.co.uk
Papers used by Vermilion are natural, recyclable products made
from wood grown in sustainable forests.

A CIP catalogue record is available for this book from the British Library.

ISBN: 0091894654

Designed and typeset by seagulls
Printed and bound in Great Britain by Clays Ltd, St Ives plc

contents

Acknowledgements

I am very grateful to the experts who gave so unstintingly of their time to help with this book. They include: Dr Linda Blair, clinical psychologist; Professor Elizabeth Chell, Director of the Institute for Entrepreneurship at Southampton University; Professor Andrew Kakabadse, Professor of International Management Development and Deputy Director of Cranfield School of Management; Dr Mark Parkinson, occupational psychologist, at the Bluewater Partnership; entrepreneur and child psychologist Pat Spungin, founder of Raisingkids.co.uk; and Murray Steele, Head of the Strategic Management Group at Cranfield School of Management.

A special thanks to: Dr Adrian Atkinson, psychologist and Managing Director of Human Factors International; and the Optomen team, especially Claire Bosworth, Debbie Christie, Olive Howe and Barbara Park.

millionaire profiles

The millionaire entrepreneurs profiled in *Think Yourself Rich*:

Alexander Amosu is the founder of RnB Ringtones and was a millionaire by the time he was 25. RnB Ringtones provides a huge variety of tunes for mobile phone rings. The company grew from nothing to a turnover of over £1 million in a year employing over a dozen staff. Alexander was awarded Young Entrepreneur of the Year at the Institute of Directors Black Enterprise Awards 2002.

Dr Adrian Atkinson is a business psychologist and founder of business consultancy Human Factors International. This company, which has advised clients as diverse as Lloyds TSB, ICI, Hilton and Powergen, specialises in focusing on the role of individuals within organisations and how their skills and personality traits can be used to maximum effect. Dr Atkinson, a millionaire and expert on the television series *Mind of a Millionaire*, has conducted large amounts of research into the qualities, aptitudes and abilities that make successful wealth creators. (For his contact details see page 218.)

Karan Bilimoria, DL owes at least some of his fortune to polo sticks. A keen polo player, he used the profit he made from selling polo sticks to Harrods to help start Cobra Beer, a beer designed specifically to go with Indian food. Karan started Cobra Beer thirteen years ago, selling his first bottles out of his dilapidated 2CV, before the bottom literally fell out. The company now has a turnover of £50 million, exports to 30 countries worldwide and the beer is sold in 5,000 Indian restaurants as well as supermarkets.

Now in his forties, Karan was brought up in India. Academically brilliant and ambitious, he started his first degree at the age of 16 in Hyderabad, following that with a career in accountancy in Britain. His boss told him to go into marketing instead and he took a law degree at Cambridge before deciding to go into business. An intensely active man who enjoys scuba diving as well as polo, he is also patron of a huge number of charities and in 2002 was named as Asian of the Year.

Robert Braithwaite, UK Entrepreneur of the Year, loves nothing more than the tang of the sea in his nostrils and the feel of the sea breeze. As owner of Britain's largest boatbuilder, Sunseeker International, he has always had a passion for boats and the ocean.

Brought up on the coast, he left school at 16 and trained as an outboard engineer. However, his dream was always to start his own boat-building company. Financed by a loan from his father's business partner, he started Sunseeker International in 1969 which now has a turnover of £130 million a year and employs over 1,000 people. Sunseeker specialises in building luxury motor boats which can cost anything from £180,000 for a streamlined speed boat to £5 million for a floating palace complete with every indulgence from designer sofas to cocktail bar and widescreen TV at the bottom of the bed. Ninety-nine per cent of the boats are exported.

Antonio and Priscilla Carluccio are a high-powered husband-and-wife team, who had formidable careers in other areas before launching their latest venture Carluccio's caffé and delicatessens. Antonio was a journalist and wine merchant before becoming a successful cook, as well as broadcasting and writing on Italian food. Priscilla has been a photographer, director of and stylist for the upmarket interiors store, the Conran Shop, and trend forecaster for the home furnishings part of the Storehouse Group. Both were already of retirement age when they decided to launch their latest entrepreneurial venture which now has 12 outlets and is growing.

William Frame, in his forties, is Director of Braemore Property Management, a highly successful Scottish property company. He started the business through a loan from the bank and with just one flat.

David Gold and his family are Britain's 67th wealthiest family, with an estimated worth of £465 million and a vast range of business interests in Gold Group International, from property to a luxury charter airline, Gold Air, and the Ann Summers chain (run by his daughter Jacqueline). He is co-owner of Birmingham City Football Club.

Chris Gorman is worth £45 million according to *The Sunday Times* Rich List. Richard Branson has named him as one of the entrepreneurs he most admires. He was co-founder of the highly successful DX Communications mobile phone group. He then launched the Reality Group, a dotcom which he sold to Great Universal Stores for a reported £35 million. He is now Executive Chairman of The Gadget Shop, which sells everything from household gadgets to novelties.

Mandy Haberman is the inventor of the Anywayup Cup, a spill-proof toddler beaker which now sells over 10 million cups a year worldwide. Mandy first became an entrepreneur when her daughter Emily was born with a feeding problem, and Mandy invented the Haberman

Feeder to ease her sucking difficulties. The success of this product encouraged Mandy to invent more and she came up with the idea for the Anywayup Cup, her most successful product to date.

Tom Hartley Senior is owner of the eponymous Tom Hartley luxury car dealership. He specialises in buying and selling top brand exclusive cars such as Ferrari, Aston Martin, Porsche and Mercedes. He sold one car for £1.2 million, the highest price ever paid for a modern car in Britain.

Tom Hartley Junior is the son of Tom Hartley Senior, above. He is now 19, and made his first million selling cars when he was just 14. He is worth an estimated £5 million and has bought himself into his father's business as a full partner.

Sahar Hashemi and her brother Bobby founded Coffee Republic, the fashionable and highly successful coffee bar credited with bringing 'skinnies' and 'lattes' to the high street. They started with one bar and grew to 100 within the first five years.

Julie Hester is founder of the Property Search Group, which runs property checks for solicitors. The business has been franchised throughout the UK with a turnover of around £25 million. It was founded in 1999. Her husband Gary is finance director.

John Madejski, OBE is currently 129th on *The Sunday Times* Rich List, worth an estimated £260 million. He devised and founded *AutoTrader*, the first UK magazine to sell used cars using photography. He now has a wide variety of business interests ranging from a hotel in the Galapagos Islands, to the Goodhead Group, a printing company that produces the telephone directory. He is probably best known for the Madejski Stadium he built for Reading Football Club, which he owns, and which also features a hotel and conference facilities.

Basil Newby had a varied career before becoming an entrepreneur, working as a Pontins Bluecoat and then starting a fancy goods store called Gone Gay. This gave him a taste for owning his own business and he started his first night club in Blackpool in 1979 with £15,000 from a brewery and a guarantee from his father, a well-known local businessman. It was the very first gay club in Blackpool, established at a time when homophobia was rife. Twenty-four years later, Basil owns six Blackpool clubs and bars, including the famous Funny Girls transvestite revue and bar. He is so well-known that many people now call Blackpool, Basil-Pool. He is estimated to be worth £15 million.

Richard Prout has launched and run several successful ventures including the hobbyists' website SmartGroups.com, which he sold to Freeserve within a year of founding it, netting £60 million. He is now again running his own company Gliant.com, which is launching a range of ventures including online gambling.

David Quayle is a serial entrepreneur best known for co-founding B&Q, the DIY Chain. When he co-founded the chain, warehouse sites were virtually unknown and you had to buy DIY equipment from builders merchants. B&Q introduced products such as Formica to the British public. David also established the Ritz video chain and has got a gallery off the ground. David left B&Q in 1982 having expanded it massively. Today B&Q and Screwfix, the mail order section, have an annual profit of £360 million

Sarah Tremellen is the founder of Bravissimo, a mail-order catalogue and retail outlet that specialises in selling lingerie to women with larger breasts. Sarah came up with the idea when she was pregnant and found there was a hugely restricted choice in larger bra sizes. She decided to launch a company specialising in supportive but attractive bras. Demand was such that, in the first year, she turned over £134,000. Eight years on, the company turns over £15 million and has over 140 staff. Sarah's husband is now her business partner.

The directors of millionaire companies profiled in *Think Yourself Rich*:

Des Benjamin is chief executive of HSA, one of Britain's major health-care providers. When he was appointed in 2000, he found an old-fashioned and hierarchical culture. Employees had to ask permission to go to the toilet and any departmental queries had to be passed through 13 layers of hierarchy. This year, HSA featured in *The Sunday Times* list of best companies to work for, winning the Well-Being Category. It has also won an award for best health care provider. Income has increased to £155 million.

Philip Williamson is Chief Executive of the Nationwide Building Society. Last year, under his leadership, profits rose by 8.5%. and assets rose to £85 billion, a 15% increase. One in four Britons uses the Nationwide for an aspect of their financial life. He started out in financial services as a Graduate Trainee for Lloyds Bank, later moving to the Nationwide as Head of Commercial Lending. He earns £838,000 a year.

introduction
– ready, steady ...

'Wealth may be an excellent thing, for it means power and it means leisure, it means liberty.'

JAMES RUSSELL LOWELL

Congratulations! By buying this book you have just taken the very first step on the road to thinking yourself rich. This is a goal that you will not achieve overnight, but it is highly achievable. The millionaires profiled in this book, and the unique survey of 300 British millionaires, the results of which are revealed here, will show you the way.

Indeed, there has never been a better time to become a self-made millionaire. When *The Sunday Times* Rich List started, most of the people on it had inherited their wealth, with self-made millionaires in the minority. Today three-quarters of those on the rich list are self-made millionaires. What's more there are 150,000 millionaires in Britain, more than ever before. When it comes to making your own million there has never been a better time to do it.

There are three ways to become rich: to inherit money, to marry money and to make money. You might well think that all three are down to luck. But you'd be wrong. While the first two are certainly a case of or right birth, or right place, right time, the third is actually far more to do with skills, values and in particular adopting a certain mindset – the mindset of a millionaire – than luck. This is good news for anyone reading this book. By taking on certain values, by living your life a particular way and by learning particular skills, you can put yourself in a great position to become wealthy.

There has never been a better time to become a millionaire

But how do we know there is what amounts to almost a formula for becoming wealthy, for developing the mind of a millionaire? It's not magic, but is based on research. This book contains perhaps the most comprehensive information ever assembled on UK millionaires, their backgrounds, their education, their careers, values, ambitions and lifestyles. Much of it is based on a survey conducted for the BBC2 series by Optomen Television, *Mind of a Millionaire*. Undertaken by the specialist agency Tulip Financial Research, which profiles millionaire spending, this fascinating survey asked 300 millionaires from all over the country about their lives. It asked them why they felt they'd been successful and about the qualities they felt had helped them achieve this success. It asked them about their childhood, whether it was happy or not, and the type of education they received. It asked them about their current lifestyles with questions ranging from the sort of house they live in, to how much they spend on the weekly supermarket shop and their favourite night out. All in all, it delved into every nook and cranny of their lives

By adopting particular values and attitudes you can learn to become rich

and backgrounds to find out what united them and if there was, indeed, a mind of a millionaire.

Their answers are highly revealing. Millionaires, for instance, did not become millionaires by lucky accident. Even from their earliest days, the survey discovered that they had ambitions to be financially secure, an ambition which was a far higher priority than, say, contributing to society or having fun. However, although the millionaires were all interested in money from a young age, they had very different levels of access to it.

Half went to state schools with half also describing themselves as having come from backgrounds that were not comfortable, or in the case of one-fifth, either poor or struggling to survive. Most had happy childhoods, but the ones who had unhappy childhoods were significantly richer and more driven, suggesting a psychological need to use their successful present to compensate for the past.

The number one ambition of millionaires was to obtain financial success

Their education varied widely too. Some millionaires were university educated, but others left school as soon as they could. (One young millionaire, profiled in chapter two, left school at the age of eleven!) Amazingly, nearly two- thirds of the millionaires were not academic achievers at school, depicting themselves as very average. (One theory is that many school under-achievers are driven to succeed in later life by their failure, another that they either have an undiagnosed problem such as dyslexia, or are simply lateral thinkers.) It was not their level of education or academic ability that made a difference to their prospects, but their attitude to both life and work, an attitude that you will learn to emulate in this book.

When it comes to how to make a million, the Tulip survey also had some original insights. You are, for instance, both more likely to become a millionaire – and richer than other millionaires – if you run your own business. However, people who made their pile working for a company or as a professional tend to be both more sociable and more easily able to switch off from work. (Your chances of making a

Many millionaires were academic under-achievers

million as a public servant are negligible with less than 10% accumulating their riches this way.) You are also far better to live in the South East or London, than say in Ulster or Wales. While the South East contains nearly a quarter of UK millionaires, Wales and Ulster have just 2%.

When it comes to lifestyles millionaires are, as you might expect, big spenders, buying huge homes, status symbol cars such as Ferraris and Bentleys (although Mercedes is, overall, the millionaire car of choice) and averaging four holidays a year. However, in some ways they are amazingly frugal. Half spend less than £500 a year on clothes, including shoes and underwear! They eschew designer stores, preferring chainstore staples such as BHS and Marks & Spencer. They also like to spend no more than £40 a head for a dinner out (roast beef is their preferred dish, way ahead of seafood or ethnic grub) and nearly a third spend less than £60 a week in the supermarket. At the same time, they also spend a great deal of their leisure time working on their investments, averaging nine hours a week, nearly as much as the average person spends watching TV!

Millionaires spend less than £500 a year on clothes but a great deal of time nurturing their investments

While millionaires' spending styles differ, so do their incomes, with the top tenth – the ultra-rich – accumulating more than £6.5 million. The ultra-rich have their own pampered and exclusive lifestyle, living in country houses, driving Rolls-Royces and holidaying at their second homes. However, there is a price for this success. They are more likely to have had a difficult childhood than the 'poorer' millionaires and more likely to be dissatisfied with their personal lives than the average millionaire. They also work harder – 64 hours a week, as opposed to the average millionaire working week of 55. They also see themselves as enthusiastic, impulsive and even aggressive. The idea of the idle rich is, it seems, totally obsolete.

Overall, the Tulip survey suggests that money *does* buy you happiness. An amazing 97% of the millionaires surveyed declared themselves to be happy with their lives. Nearly half were very happy indeed. This compares with a UK average of 85% (happy) a third (very happy). The idea that money brings happiness is also reinforced by a survey of lottery winners conducted by MORI. Seventy per cent of the winners felt the windfall had improved their lives. A further 28% were just as happy as they had been before. People who are wealthy are less buffeted by outside forces and more able to steer their own destiny – and research shows that being in control of our lives is a major factor for happiness.

Being in control of your life is a major factor in achieving happiness

Indeed, you could even say that money gives you a better relation ship with your partner. Contrary to the general view of millionaires as 'playboys', most British and US millionaires have been very happily married to their first wife for over 15 years (85% of British millionaires are men and this increases to 97% in the US).

Above all, being rich in our society is a measure of success. In virtually all jobs and businesses, money is the reward for success. Do you know anyone who was paid less the more successful they became? Success and being rich are often the same thing.

But what does all this mean to you? From where you are standing now, struggling to pay off your credit card debt, start a business or simply have a better standard of living, being successful or becoming a millionaire can seem as far away as the outer reaches of the solar system. You may already be feeling, as you read this introduction, that you have bitten off more than you can chew and that talking about millions is irrelevant when the only millions you possess seem to be millions of problems!

Most British millionaires are happily married to their first wives

You could, of course, enter the lottery. Ironically, though, the way that most people try to become millionaires is the strategy that is least likely to succeed: the odds of winning the jackpot in any week are 14 million to one, which means your chances of being murdered are considerably higher. It could be you. But it probably won't be.

You could also try going on the famous game show 'Who Wants to Be a Millionaire' – but there have been very few legitimate winners in the show's history.

No, the surest way to become rich, these days, is to earn it. To inspire you, this book contains profiles of wealthy people who have made their money entirely through their own efforts, rather than through inheritance or a jackpot win. Indeed, none of the people interviewed in this book started out wealthy. Some dropped out of school, failed their exams or have had business failures. All of them have had times when they have struggled. Like rock climbers, they have been left dangling off the ledge before they reached their summit. Some have had to work 80 hours a week, seemingly without getting anywhere, before they realised their dream. Indeed, one multimillionaire, Chris Gorman, compares business success to an old-fashioned water pump. He points out that it takes huge amounts of effort to get a water pump started, then you pump and pump for ages, before the first drop and trickle creak and grind their way through. However, once that first trickle of water comes through, the rest flows more easily, first steadily and then faster. It is all a question of momentum. But if you do not take the first step – start the pump going – then you will never reap the rewards.

The odds of winning the jackpot in any week are over 14 million to one

None of the millionaires in this book started out wealthy

The millionaires whose inspiring stories feature in this book come from a huge variety of fields ranging from motorboats and luxury cars, to retailers and dotcom wizards. They range in age from one who made his first million at 14 (and is currently 19), to several in their sixties, and in assets from several million to several hundred million. Most are men, but a few are women, reflecting the national millionaire profile. Whatever your experience, aptitude, age, gender and ethnicity, you are likely to find people whose experience speaks directly to you and whose story ignites your own enthusiasm to succeed.

'It's like a water pump. You have to do a lot of pumping before the first drops of water come out, but those drops turn to a steady flow. Growing a business is like that.' CHRIS GORMAN

Indeed, some of you could be just a few years away from becoming seriously wealthy. While it takes an average of 20 years to accumulate a million pounds' worth of assets, some of the millionaires profiled here have achieved multimillion pound success in a much shorter period, in one case less than a year! To follow their example, you need to learn their lessons and establish your own blueprint making sure to absorb the values and ethos – the mind of a millionaire – described here.

Of course, reading this book alone won't make you a millionaire. If only it were that simple! If you are a classroom teacher who loves what you do and are content to stay inside the classroom, you need to accept that you will never make a million from the day job, however inspired your teaching.

Nevertheless, even if there is a salary ceiling on the day job, you will learn in this book not only how to maximise your earning potential within your day job, but how to enhance your earnings and saving potential outside it. At its simplest, a teacher could, for instance,

You will learn to maximise your earnings and earning potential

develop a strategy to use evenings and holidays to offer private tuition and use this money as part of a saving and investment strategy. Over time this would enable him to achieve a more comfortable lifestyle than colleagues relying solely on their pay cheque and pension. He might even decide to start his own tutorial agency, a move which could yield major profit. Then again, he might decide that becoming seriously wealthy means changing priorities he isn't willing to change. Whichever decision he makes he will have learnt something enormously valuable.

This book will help you decide how much you want to prioritise wealth-making in your life and what changes to your lifestyle you are willing to make to think yourself rich.

Whether you are a small-business owner who wants to grow, a prospective entrepreneur looking to start a business, someone who wants to climb the corporate tree or, indeed, someone who hasn't yet decided which direction to take, this book has insights for you. It will be equally valuable if *You may need to change your priorities if you want to become seriously wealthy* you are struggling with debts, or merely discontented with your life, wanting to become wealthier, but not sure how. It is time to learn to think yourself rich. After that, it's down to you to put these exciting lessons into daily practice.

making a start

the basics of thinking yourself rich

'Never turn down a job because you think it's too small. You don't know where it can lead.'
JULIA MORGAN

'If I can do it, you can do it.'
ALEXANDER AMOSU, A SELF-MADE MILLIONAIRE BY THE TIME HE WAS 25

You want to be richer. Here's how you make a valuable start. This goal is achievable, but that doesn't mean there is a quick-fix solution, or that it will happen overnight. All the millionaires interviewed for this book mentioned the word *sacrifice* at least once.

If you are serious about fulfilling your potential and making more money, you will need to be prepared to change the way you live. You must adopt different priorities, goals and expectations of yourself and others. You will need to emphasise some of your qualities and minimise others. You might have to rethink your values, how you spend your time and how much time you devote to, say, reading the sports pages of the newspaper as opposed to the money and business pages. Some of these adjustments may be easy.

Others will be more difficult. How much or how little you decide to do will depend largely on your own ambition, motivation and priorities. Put simply, it is a lot easier to increase your wealth by £10,000 than by £100,000, a lot easier to aim to be moderately rich than hugely so. What you have to decide is what success means to you – and how much you are prepared to change your life to get it.

You will need different priorities, different goals and different expectations of yourself and others

Do remember though, that being rich cannot be the be-all and end-all of your ambition. How you become rich and the enjoyment you have pursuing the journey is just as important as the end itself. Even when you are rich, how you feel about and how you spend the money is as important as the money itself. You could choose to lock up every spare penny over £20,000 in a large vault, but it would be neither a good investment nor much fun.

Being rich is, in itself, not sufficient ambition. That's because we all have very different ideas of what rich actually is. Indeed, the amazing thing about being rich is that the rich are always people who have more money than you have now. You will find that if your current definition of rich is, say, £50,000 a year, once you achieve that income your definition will be at least twice that! It is more important to work out what you want the money for, and how it will change your life, than just to pluck a figure out of thin air.

A few of you will read this book and decide that although you admire the wealthy and successful people portrayed here, you do not want to make the sacrifices they made, or mirror their priorities. If so, you will have learnt something valuable about yourself and will be able to focus on your priorities without the envy and sour grapes that comes from believing you could do it too, if only you could be bothered. Understanding why you don't want to be, or simply cannot be, as successful as some of the people featured here, will make you more contented.

On the other hand, one of the most encouraging things about writing this book is that the millionaires themselves believe that anyone can become wealthy if they want to do so badly enough.

So how do you get started on this roller-coaster journey? In this chapter, we give you some of the foundations for future success. Take your time doing the exercises and quizzes that you find here as they will affect both your future choices and lifestyle.

you can do it – believe you can

The success stories encountered in the course of researching this book were all very different. They come from different parts of the country, from middle-class, or poor backgrounds, some were university educated, others left school as early as 11. They have different personalities too. Some are loud and outgoing, the life and soul of the party, others much quieter and more contemplative. However, whatever their background and personality, all had one major factor in common: they believed, often from a very young age, that they would and could be successful. All of them wanted to make something of their lives, believed in themselves and felt they would win through.

Self-belief is crucial in anyone who intends to be successful. Becoming successful is challenging and difficult and if you are filled with doubts about your ability, even before you start, you are under a tremendous handicap. It is like trying to run the 100 metres with your legs tied together.

What's more, if you don't believe in yourself, why on earth should anyone else? People take you largely at your own valuation and if you see yourself as a failure, then it's hard to see how they will see you as a success.

learn from the millionaires

When John Madejski was a boy, schoolmates teased him about his foreign name (taken from his stepfather) and few people could spell it. Today the laugh is on them. Not only is John extremely rich, he also has a stadium in Reading, his home town, funded by and named after him (Madejski stadium), a gallery in the local museum (the John Madejski gallery) and a lecture theatre (you can guess the title). 'A lot more people can spell my name now,' he says. He is also the owner of Reading Football Club although, oddly, he isn't a football fanatic. It seems to have been a case of *noblesse oblige* – no one else was willing to buy it – but his purchase of the club has made him something of a local hero.

Given the teasing John endured at school, it's not surprising that he was determined to succeed, a determination increased by the fact that he was no academic star at school. 'I beat myself up about my lack of prowess at school for a long time,' he says. 'My contemporaries went to university, I went off around the world.'

He also knew that he wanted to run his own show, but finding the right idea was much trickier. As a classified ad salesman on a newspaper, he began to work out which businesses succeeded – and why – but he couldn't find the killer concept. Even worse, he began to have burning chest and stomach pains that turned out to be anxiety pangs, caused by sheer frustration.

Then he saw a US car magazine that used crude photography. This was the revelation he'd been waiting for. He returned home confident that, this time, he'd found a concept that would work. But knowing something is right and getting others to take it seriously are two different things. 'It was like pushing a ball continually uphill, but it had to work,' he says. This single-minded determination paid off. He set up *AutoTrader* for £2,000 and worked furiously to get it off the ground, using photography and slick layout. Just over 20 years later, he sold it and the publishing group he'd built around it, for £260 million, netting himself £174 million.

If you wish to be successful, then you will need grit, determination and an ability to ignore the doubters. If you do not believe in yourself sufficiently it is doubtful that you will come through. Indeed, academic research shows that there is a strong correlation between self-belief and achievement. A case of 'I think, therefore I am'.

If you don't believe in yourself, why should anyone else?

It is the belief that they can – and will – succeed that has not only motivated the people interviewed in this book but has sustained them through very difficult times, the times when they had no money, the business was failing or when they didn't get the break they deserved.

Their self-belief has also meant that they have pursued an idea, or career path, even if others were positively incredulous at the idea it would work. Many of the millionaires interviewed said that their initial brilliant idea was met with sighs, raised eyebrows or cries of 'it won't work', by well-meaning friends and colleagues. Nevertheless, they carried on, often in the teeth of opposition. As Dr Adrian Atkinson, Managing Director of Human Factors International, the business psychology strategy firm, remarks: 'These are people who didn't know it was impossible – so they did it.' This is the nub of the millionaire mindset – self-belief, despite the odds.

'These are people who didn't know it was impossible, so they did it.'
DR ADRIAN ATKINSON

Such self-belief and confidence are invaluable in creating success. Many of you reading this book may, in your heart, believe you don't have what it takes to start a business, climb the corporate ladder or become rich. If you believe that, you won't get there. It is vital not only that you believe that you can be richer and more successful, but that you actually have enough self-confidence to do what it takes.

set your goals

Of course, it is easy to state that self-belief is vital. It is, however, far harder to gain it. Even if you tell yourself every day (and you certainly should) that you can and will succeed, it can sometimes be difficult to truly believe it. So how do you bolster your own confidence and self-belief?

'If you have faith in your idea and your abilities then you will gain self-belief.'

Karan Bilimoria

Dr Adrian Atkinson believes that one of the best ways of shoring up self-belief and simultaneously taking the first step to success is to view your life as a project, with you as project manager in chief. As in every good project, you need to have a clear, overarching vision of what you want to achieve, broken down into smaller goals, or milestones. At this point, it's a good idea to start with a 10-year plan or even, if you are sure of what you want, a 20-year plan. However, do remember that if you set yourself a 20-year plan, your goals might well change as your experience does. For instance, if you are 20 now, having a happy family life may feature extremely low on the list, but much higher when you are 40. When you think of long-term goals, it helps to be flexible. When it comes to short-term goals, i.e. next week or next month, it helps to be very specific and targeted.

The advantages of goal-setting are:

- It gives you a clear vision of what matters to you in life and what you want to aim for.

- It gives you a good idea of what you can achieve and, just as important, how to go about it today, next week and next year.

- It enables you to focus clearly on your vision and helps avoid you being blown off course entirely by outside events or other distractions.

🌓 It helps you decide what is right for you, not what other people decide is right for you.

🌓 It enables you to set priorities down to a day-to-day, hour-to-hour level. For instance, you may weigh social events against your goal-setting and decide, for instance, to attend one party because it allows you to network with people who might contribute to your goals, but avoid another and work instead because it is irrelevant to your goals.

🌓 It builds your confidence and self-belief as you achieve your goals and set new ones. Even if you do not achieve all your goals you will undoubtedly have achieved more for having set them than those who have just drifted with the tide. This in itself gives confidence.

🌓 It promotes clear, focused thinking and gives you motivation even on bad days and when times are tough. It gives you the gift of self-analysis so that you are continually improving.

🌓 It helps you avoid getting in a rut. People with goals do not get stuck in a permanent comfort zone, vaguely discontented but not sure what to do about it. Having goals helps you decide when it is time to go for promotion, change job or start up a business.

🌓 It builds self-esteem. As children we often receive stickers or certificates for milestones achieved, good performance at school or sports matches won. As adults, there are very few 'certificates' for good performance. Goal-setting enables you to celebrate your successes.

Goal-setting is easy as long as you know what your eventual aim is. It is, for instance, much easier for a football team to set out with the aim of moving up a division, or winning the premiership, than to merely hope to win each game and see how it goes. In order to set really effective long-term goals you need to know just what really matters to you, what your dreams and priorities are.

This is where it pays to dream. If you could achieve one thing in life, what would it be? Be realistic, though – there is no point wanting to be a premiership footballer if you never made the first eleven in the school team and are now 30!

Look at your talents, your skills, the things you have done before and really enjoyed and ask yourself how you can use these previous experiences to create real goals for yourself. For instance, Karan Bilimoria knew that he wanted to run a

> '**To be successful you need to have a goal and work hard enough and long enough at it.**'
> TOM HARTLEY JUNIOR, BRITAIN'S YOUNGEST SELF-MADE MILLIONAIRE

business. His first attempt – selling polo sticks – was moderately successful. However, it was only when he came up with the idea of Cobra Beer, a concept he knew could succeed internationally, that he was able to focus both on the short-term goal of getting it off the ground and then the longer-term goal of build-

This is where it pays to dream

ing an international brand.

To help make your goals more concrete, try the exercise opposite. Then set down your ten-year goal. Think about it carefully and make sure you are happy with it. After all, it will determine much of your life.

Be as explicit as possible. For instance, saying that you want to be a managing director of a firm could cover a whole host of possibilities. These range from running your own one-man corner shop to becoming managing director of BP or running your own retail empire. If you want to run your own business, for instance, how big will it be? Will you end up with one shop or many? Will it be the foremost in its field? Ideally, if you already have knowledge or even a particular interest in a certain area, you should try to build your goal around that. Remember, in order to really invest in your goal, you need both to

exercise: defining the dream

On a blank sheet of paper, or in a notebook, have a go at answering the questions below. This will help you clarify where your real priorities and strengths lie.

1 When you were a child, how did you see yourself as an adult? Is that how you see yourself now?

2 Have you achieved what you wanted to achieve by this age? If not, in what areas are you lacking – in career, in your personal life, in financial terms?

3 Where does your greatest source of happiness come from: your career? your major relationship? your hobbies? your social life? Place these in order of priority. Then ask yourself: does your life reflect your priorities? If not, what do you need to change and how can you do that? Be honest, do not put that your family comes first if actually you are desperate to get back to the office by Monday morning.

4 What did you most enjoy at school? What were you best at? And what part of your job gives you most fulfilment now?

5 What did you least like and enjoy at school? And now?

6 What are your skills?

7 What are you weak at?

8 How do you see yourself in five years' time ... and in ten?

9 How would you *like* to be in five years' time ... and in ten?

10 How do your two versions differ?

learn from the millionaires

Karan Bilimoria owes at least part of his fortune to polo sticks. A talented polo player (he was a Cambridge blue, as well as a keen scuba diver), his first idea for a business was to sell pukha polo sticks to Harrods. The money he made from that helped him start Cobra.

Not that Karan had seemed to be destined for life as a business-man. Urbane, fastidious and academically brilliant, he won a place at Hyderabad University at 15, then studied accountancy in Britain. Realising a life of figures wasn't likely to hold his attention, he opted for a law degree at Cambridge, funding it through auditing accounts. It was then that his big idea began to take shape.

Pining for the sort of homely Indian cooking he was used to, he ate out regularly and noticed that there was a lamentable lack of a beer that suited Indian cuisine. A combination of spicy food and conventional gassy beer meant diners felt bloated quickly, finishing neither their food nor drink. Karan felt sure there was a market for a less gassy beer. 'I even had the taste in my mouth,' he recalls.

He was sure his concept would be a winner. His family were not. They felt he should stick to a profession. So did Mysore Breweries, the biggest Indian brewery, when he contacted them with his eureka idea, no track record and no funding. 'When I arrived, the whole management team were there and most of them laughed in my face,' he recalls. They told Karan how their competitors had also wanted to export Indian beer to Britain and most had come a cropper. 'I didn't stand a chance, according to them,' Karan recalls. 'I told them that all their competitors had lacked one thing – me. I told them I believed in myself, in the product and that I would make it happen. If you have faith in your idea and abilities, then you gain self-belief.'

believe in it and feel passionately about it. In life, sticking to what you care about and are skilled at can take you a long way.

You may, of course, be largely content with your life but need extra income for a certain project – buying a house, for instance, or getting out of debt. This involves setting much shorter goals than a ten-year plan. In your case, you may want to set a realistic framework for getting out of debt, or buying a house within a specific time frame. Saying you will get out of debt, or buy a house, is simply not specific enough. Once you have achieved that goal, you can set the next.

Be precise when deciding your goals

If your goal is to buy a house, do not just write down 'buy house'. Instead, write down what sort of home you think you can buy within the time period you have set yourself. For instance, you may want to buy a three-bedroom, semi-detached home in a particular area. That way you know what you are aiming for. Do not set your sights too low. 'Any rundown old pile that I can just about afford with a few well-placed lies to the building society' is not a real goal.

It's essential that you care about what you do

At the same time, do not be unrealistic. A stately home by this time next year is not a realistic goal for someone currently living in a council house. Goals should always be, in management-speak, SMART: specific, measurable, achievable, realistic and timed.

Consult friends and close family about your vision. If you have a partner they will need to understand and buy into your vision too

Consult friends and close family about your vision. If, for instance, you have a partner, they will need to buy into your vision too. If you don't have a partner, you may want to consider whether finding one is an important part of your life vision – and the time you will need to devote to that. Or whether this is incidental to your dreams.

Think about what, who and how much you would be prepared to sacrifice to reach your goal. Will those sacrifices be worth it if you get there?

Once you have a detailed, highly individual vision of what success in 10 or 20 years' time means to you, you can now start to implement it.

'I have written goals. I also review my time each hour, each day. Of course, I always cram more in than I can do, so I run late. But at the end of each day, I do look back and ask, what have I done today, what have I accomplished?'
KARAN BILIMORIA

your long-term goals

Show your ten-year goal to your closest friends or family whom you trust and who already believe in you. Do they think you are under-achieving? Should you be more ambitious?

1 **Now divide your ambitions into five-year increments.** This is so that you have a clear route that will allow you to reach your goal. All you have to do now is follow the path.

Now you need to break down your first goal into small, achievable steps. Ask yourself:

2 **'What can I do this week to take the first steps towards my goal?'** Set achievable, concrete steps and tick them off as you achieve them. For instance, if your goal is to set up your own business, this week's challenge may be to find out and note down all the possible sources of funding. If you want to become MD of your company, finding out about the next steps for promotion, or training courses, may be a good first step.

3 **What can you do within a fortnight? A month? A year?** Gradually increase your aims and scope of your goals. You will find that, as you succeed, your confidence grows and you are able to increase the challenges you set for yourself. Do not be put off by the odd setback or failure. These are inevitable. Just reframe your goals and start over.

If you fail to succeed in one goal, do not stop goal-setting or trying to achieve your goals. This is like a football team withdrawing from the league because they lost a match. Many sportsmen go on to become great entrepreneurs. They know that if things go wrong you have to pick yourself up and keep going. However, if you consistently do not reach your goals, you may need either to reframe your goals or try harder. If you do not reach a goal within the allotted time-frame, analyse in depth what went wrong. Was the goal too ambitious? Did you put in too little effort? Do you need to take a slightly different course to reach your goal?

If you are not sure about your long-term goal, do not abandon this project. Instead, set a short-term goal (say, enough money for a holiday or a car) over the next year, work out how to achieve it and then set a new goal when you reach the first. The long-term goal may well become clear to you as you start to take control of your life and realise what your priority really is and where your skills lie. It is important, however, to set realistic and achievable goals and to break them into small steps so that you do not get discouraged.

You may want to use a mental picture of yourself running a business, or as a senior manager. If there is a particular manager whose job you would like, imagine yourself in that role. If your primary goal is to earn a certain amount, or to afford a certain car, within a year, then keep a picture of that car on your wall or in your wallet to motivate you.

Motivation, of course, is a key factor. So each goal should also have an in-built reward for reaching it. This may be as little as, say, a good bottle of wine for keeping a month's goal, to buying a Mercedes or

BMW or a slap-up holiday if you achieve your five-year plan. Again, keeping a picture of the 'reward' object may help you focus better on your goal and prevent you from being distracted.

Do not be put off if you fail to reach a particular goal by a certain

learn from the millionaires

For Sahar Hashemi, a high-heeled whirlwind of a woman and co-founder of Coffee Republic, it was a stay in New York, as a high-powered lawyer, that stimulated her love affair with coffee. She revelled in the different varieties and the fat-free muffins that helped her retain her trim, mini-skirted figure. Back in London, however, coffee was served instant, slopped over the saucer and sold as an adjunct to sandwiches.

Lamenting to her brother Bobby the loss of her lattes, he suggested that introducing such coffee bars to Britain would be a tremendous hit. Sahar took some persuading, even telling Bobby she'd be happy just to be his first regular customer! However, she soon began to be revved up by the idea, literally, as one research trip involved a tour of as many coffee bars in New York as she could drink in. (One astute manager even spotted that she was idea-hunting and chased her off the premises.)

As someone with professional experience as a lawyer (including serving a writ on miners' leader Arthur Scargill), but with no business experience, Sahar found setting goals for the business really helped her get it off the ground and deal with the vast, fast expansion. 'I always thought it was important to set goals,' says Sahar. 'We had a vision of a finished product that kept us going, but it was important to have those goals to be able to achieve it. I think it's important to review goals every six months because everything around you changes and you have to adapt to that.'

time if, for instance, illness or a downturn in the market occurs. Just reframe your time-scale. Giving up because you haven't attained a particular goal is like a dieter reaching for the chocs just because they haven't hit a particular weight. Steady effort is as important as reaching the target on time. Again, if you continually fail to hit any targets, think about reframing the targets to make them more realistic and achievable.

Many people find that continually picturing their goal helps them keep sharply focused on it

The easiest way is to keep a chart listing in detail what you want to achieve. The exercise on page 30 will help you do this.

being focused

One of the questions that people commonly ask is 'Are millionaires selfish?' The answer is both no – and yes. Many of the individuals interviewed for this book are extremely public-spirited. They work for charities, they are involved in community organisations ranging from children's charities to the local Parent-Teacher Association. Karan Bilimoria, for instance, educates the children of widows in India and is patron of several charities including unfashionable ones, such as Rethink for people with severe mental illness. Chris Gorman gives considerable time and funds to charities that range from the Princess Royal Trust for Carers to NCH (formerly National Children's Homes). John Madejski has endowed a Madejski Gallery to The Royal Academy London and one to Reading, as well as a lecture theatre.

However, the millionaires were selfish in one sense. They had their goals, priorities, vision, and none of them had allowed themselves to be blown off course by others' priorities, others' expectations of them or the wish to kowtow to others' demands. In other words, they were self-motivated, rather than motivated by praise, or the need to be loved. They pursued their own objectives, rather than trying to fit

exercise: your goal chart

1 On a blank piece of paper fill out this chart and all the charts below, and answer the questions raised as you reach each stage:

What I want to achieve this week	My reward will be
My career	
My lifestyle	
My personal life	

- What did I do well last week?
- What could I have improved?
- What first step will I take this week to take me towards my major goal? Write down at least two but no more than five actions.
- What will I do to take me towards my other goals? Write down no more than two actions.
- What are my next steps?
- How can I improve the way I am proceeding towards my goals?

What I want to achieve in a fortnight	My reward will be
My career	
My lifestyle	
My personal life	

- Am I making the progress I have set for myself?
- What more can I do?
- What am I doing well? What am I doing not well enough?
- Do I have sufficient motivation?
- What can I do to increase motivation?

What I want to achieve in a month's time	My reward will be
My career	
My lifestyle	
My personal life	

- Am I on track with my goals?
- Can I congratulate myself on my progress?
- Can I increase the scope of my goals, set them higher?
- What have I learnt so far?
- What have I done well, and what not so well?
- What are the next steps I need to take?

What I want to achieve in six months' time	My reward will be
My career	
My lifestyle	
My personal life	

- Is my motivation flagging? What can I do to motivate myself?
- Have I met unexpected obstacles? How have I tackled them?
- Have I had unexpected successes? What have I learnt?
- Do I need to repeat my visualisation?
- Can I give myself a reward?
- Have I looked at how far I have come since I started approaching this exercise?
- Have I met any of my goals? How far from them am I?

What I want to achieve in a year's time	My reward will be
My career	
My lifestyle	
My personal life	

- Have I met my year goal? If not, why not?
- What can I do to meet the goal or do I need to adapt it?
- What have I done well this year?
- What can I improve?
- If I've met my year goal, I will enjoy my reward.
- If I've not met the goal, I will either meet the goal soon, or I need to reframe it.

Tip: Try visualising how you will feel when you reach your first year goal and reward. Now imagine the reward and imagine yourself at this level. How do you feel? Use this feeling to help you propel yourself towards your goals.

What I want to achieve in five years' time	My reward will be
My career	
My lifestyle	
My personal life	

- Have I met my five-year goal? If not, why not?
- Were the circumstances that prevented me meeting my goal beyond my control (e.g. illness, family crisis), or could I have handled my life better to meet my goal?
- What can I do to meet the goal or do I need to adapt it to take account of my changed life?
- What have I done well during these years?
- What can I improve?
- If I've met my goal, what reward did I promise myself? When can I enjoy it?

What I want to achieve in ten years' time	My reward will be
My career	
My lifestyle	
My personal life	

2 Constantly review your goals and update them at least each month. Insert timings if that helps you. For instance, 'This week I will spend five hours getting my finances sorted.'

You will notice that the goal-setting is especially detailed in the first year. This is because it takes a while to get into the mindset of goal-setting, rewarding and achieving. If you do well in your first year, however, you will find it much easier to manage your goals in the second year and, by the third year, goal-setting, self-analysis and reviewing your goals will become automatic to you.

them around the objectives of others. Trying to please everyone is after all, a recipe for pleasing no one, especially yourself.

Successful people are single-minded. They have goals and pursue them vigorously. They do not allow themselves to be shipwrecked on the rocks of others' opinions of them or their ideas, or what they should or shouldn't do.

It's one thing to say no to an acquaintance. It's another thing to say no to your partner, parents or children. You need to decide just how much you will give up to win your prize. In medieval literature, a common theme is the knight who sets off on a quest. Sometimes it's for the Holy Grail, sometimes it's to rescue a princess. Along the way, he faces all sorts of trials, temptations, mirages and spirits. Sometimes he is injured or

Successful people are not hindered by the opinions of others

loses an eye or his favourite horse or dog. He always succeeds, but the cost is high. You need to decide how much pain you are prepared to take on your own personal quest. If you know beforehand what you are prepared to give up you will have fewer regrets later on. Here is something to help you think about this:

how much do your goals mean to you?

What would I be willing to sacrifice to obtain these goals?

- In my weekly goals would I be willing to give up: a night out, a party, a dinner with my spouse, much of my leisure time this week?
- In my six-monthly to yearly goals would I be prepared to give up: a holiday, a friendship, the approval of my colleagues?
- In my yearly to five-yearly goals would I be prepared to give up: my relationship, my friendships? Which ones?

Know your limits so you know the sacrifices you are prepared to make and those you are not.

thinking about your money style

It's great to set goals, but the knack is to actually achieve them. All too often people set either limited goals for themselves, or sabotage their own goals through lack of focus, allowing themselves to be diverted or even going off course. So why is it that although so many people claim they want or need a certain lifestyle, income or status, so few of them actually achieve it?

T. Harv Eker is a business guru famous throughout North America for his seminars on creating wealth. He believes that it is often people's subconscious that stops them becoming wealthy or successful. While they may consciously tell themselves they want to be rich or successful, their subconscious shies away, telling them that

learn from the millionaires

When Chris Gorman isn't working he paces around his sound studio and disco at his home with the 'energy of a hyperactive eight-year-old'. Like Tigger, he is always on the go whether it's making back-to-back phone calls as he is chauffeured from meeting to meeting, partying with friends or trying out the latest gadgets from The Gadget Shop. (Both he and his children are gadget fanatics.)

His millionaire lifestyle is a whole world away from his impoverished childhood. He was considered lucky when, at the age of 16, he landed a job in the local supermarket, although he asserts luck had nothing to do with it. He'd had a part-time job with them and was actually working for the company while sitting his exams! 'I'd look at the manager there who was earning £30,000 a year in his mid-thirties and think, maybe I could do that.' Then he read a self-help book, *How to Win Friends and Influence People* by Dale Carnegie, which made him question whether he could actually achieve more.

He became a highly successful salesperson, eventually moving to London. However, when his vivacious blonde wife, Mary, became pregnant, they decided to move to Scotland to be near family. They had to sell their house at a loss and left, £30,000 in debt, starting their new life in a council house. It was then that Chris feels his goal-setting kicked in with a vengeance. Having had a taste of money, he was determined to make it again. 'We'd go and look at show-homes every weekend, so we could see the house we wanted to move to. It's like offering a kid sweets, then taking them away. It makes you want it more.'

Having the vision of the house he wanted helped him stay focused. As soon as they'd managed to move into the first house, they took to looking at show-homes again, looking for the second home to act as an incentive. This worked so well that the Gormans moved five times in five years, each time to a better property. He now lives in a house where the master bedroom is about the same size as that entire council house!

they can't be that rich, or that they are not bright enough to make it, ensuring that they somehow sabotage themselves to satisfy their subconscious urges.

But why would anyone avoid being wealthy and successful? There are several possible reasons:

1 Social attitudes. We live in a society that has a strangely ambiguous attitude towards money. On the one hand, we admire the rich for being rich, on the other we are enormously suspicious of wealth and wealth creation. Think of the sayings associated with wealth: 'filthy rich', 'money doesn't buy happiness', 'more money than sense', 'money is the root of all evil', 'you can't take it with you'.

Indeed, although we both admire – and envy – those who have wealth, our society is also very suspicious of it, often labelling rich people as 'crooks' or 'ruthless', simply because they have been successful. If you feel, deep down, that being rich isn't a worthwhile goal, then you will subconsciously refuse to make the effort to be rich. You have to believe that being rich is important, to put the effort in.

2 We are hugely influenced by our parents' attitude to money and success. If we grew up in a household where our parents threw money around, we are likely to emulate them. If we grew up in a household where money was always tight and a source of misery and frustration, we are likely to have a view of money as destructive. If we grew up indulged, we may always choose to indulge ourselves, even when we cannot afford it. If money came easily we assume it will always come easily. If money was a taboo subject, then we are also likely to be reluctant to talk about it. Sometimes we are even influenced without realising it.

'It's possible to react against a certain money style,' says Dr Pat Spungin, child psychologist and entrepreneurial founder of www.raisingkids.co.uk. 'For instance, if your parents always complain about the price of everything or that everything is poor

learn from the millionaires

Tom Hartley Senior has a pristine home and the sort of extensive garden that could easily accommodate a tennis court or a swimming pool with patio. But Tom has something very different. In his garden, instead of garden furniture and statues sit a row of the sort of cars that car enthusiasts faint over. Gleaming Ferraris, sleek, sophisticated Aston Martins, curvaceous Porsches and classic Mercedes.

For Tom, a forthright, forceful man, making money – and the control it gives him over his own life – is hugely important. 'For the first 20 years of running the business I never remember a day when I didn't wake up and think about making money that day. And I mean *never*.'

Tom has delivered cars on Christmas Day. He has driven his gleaming beasts through the night to the other end of the country when a client has wanted a 2 a.m. delivery at the end of a party.

He's equally driven when it comes to finding the right car to sell. He has dived into saunas in luxury spas to find the owner of a car parked outside, or negotiated at the reception desks of hotels when a certain car has caught his eye. 'Everywhere and anywhere is a good way to do business,' he says.

Owning a luxury-car dealership is many a small boy's dream. But despite being a multimillionaire, Tom is also happy to roll up his sleeves and wash a car if one needs cleaning up. He believes that when it comes to making money, you have to be prepared to do the work, whether glamorous or not. Being arrogant, or precious, doesn't pay.

Tom is dismissive of those who believe money isn't important. 'Critics would say money isn't everything. All I would say to that is that everything seems to be money wherever I go.' He is also adamant that making money isn't the breeze people seem to think it is. 'The first £100, the first £1,000, the first million is always the hardest.'

He also points out that one of his favourite maxims is a pound saved is a pound earned. 'A lot of people spend extravagantly when times are good and then wish they'd saved it later when times are bad,' he says. 'If you don't waste it, you won't want for it.'

tips to bolster your self-esteem

1 Write down all your good qualities. Write down things that you are especially proud of as well as good things that others have said about you which have made you proud.

2 Write down a list of your successes since childhood, no matter how minor.

3 Resolve to tell yourself each morning that you can – and will – succeed. Remind yourself that you are a valuable person. Look at your goals each week and month.

4 If you feel you have made a right decision, but it has led you into conflict with someone else, remind yourself that this is *their* problem.

5 Do not be overly modest. There is no point slogging away hoping someone/anyone will spot your brilliance. They won't, or they might and merely take credit for it themselves. They may not even realise what a brilliant job you are doing. After all, how can they know how many problems you have solved unless you tell them? It's the same as visiting the doctor. If the doctor gives you a pill and you go away, he can't possibly know that the remedy has failed unless you tell him. If you have found a brilliant way around a thorny work problem, don't just tell your colleagues, tell your boss. If a customer praises you, ask the customer to let your boss know too. If you receive a letter of thanks for your work, for goodness' sake, show it off. This doesn't mean you have to become boastful, it means rather that you need to cannily select whom it is important to tell in order to advance your career.

6 Dress for success. It's a cliché, but it's important. You will not make it to the board of an investment bank dressed in Mr Byrite and sporting a tattoo on your face, however brilliant your financial insights. Nor are you likely to wow them at interviews with piercings sprouting from every available pore. (Ignore this advice if you are a woman looking for a career in lap dancing.) Look at the successful people in your organisation or the area in which you want to work. How do they dress? What is their style? How do their clothes denote status? Observe them carefully and then copy them. Style consultants often say that you should dress for the rank above yours. Once you are the Chair you can express yourself through your clothing but, by that time, the chances are that expressing yourself will mean dressing the way most successful directors, business people or professionals do. Sad, but true.

value, you may decide to do the opposite but you are still being influenced by them.'

In the main, we inherit the money attitudes of the household in which we grew up. If money was well-managed, we tend to be good money managers. If money was a source of joy and celebration, then we tend to have positive associations with it. It is attitudes towards money, rather than the income level of the household, that determines our values. Many of the people in this book came from families where the work ethic was highly valued and where they were expected to help pay their way from a young age. Most of them yearned for a higher

exercise: your attitude to money

Think about the following:

1   If I imagine myself as wealthy, how do I imagine myself? What sort of life would I lead?

2   Do I believe one can be too rich?

3   If I think about rich people, what words spring to mind?

4   Do I regard money as a source of joy, satisfaction and fulfilment? Do I see it as my enemy, something that always defeats and frustrates me, and that makes me miserable? Or is it a necessary evil?

5   In what ways would money improve my life? And in what ways would money have a negative influence? How important or beyond my control are those negative influences?

6   What was my family's attitude towards money when I was growing up? How did my parents relate to money? Were they in control of their money, or did it control them? How am I following that pattern? How do I want to change it?

7   What are my spending strengths and weaknesses?

8   How will greater income and success enhance my life?

9   Re-examine negative feelings about money (after all, wealth itself, can be either morally good or morally bad, depending on what you do with it).

10   Once you have thought about your attitude towards money and how your childhood has influenced it, think about how you will consciously change that attitude (e.g. if you have been a heavy spender, how you will consciously learn to manage your money).

standard of living and greater financial security. By rating money and work highly, they were ideally placed to become successful. To find out your subconscious attitude towards money try the exercise on page 40.

Even if your family were always careless with money and you have been the same, it is possible to change your behaviour. You just have to make a conscious – and constant – effort to be different from your parents and to hold different values and take different actions. It is our choices, not our backgrounds, that define who we become.

learning to be money-wise

In most fields, if you are successful, you will be financially rewarded and will receive a high salary. If you run a successful business, you will either award yourself a good salary, or even sell out for a high price. But a high income is not the same as being rich. It is incredibly easy to spend and even waste the money you earn, as various pools winners and former footballers can attest.

You might think that millionaires would be lavish with their money, throwing it around as if it were as plentiful as summer weeds. In fact, the opposite is true. Millionaires are actually extremely careful with their money. The Tulip survey revealed that nearly half spent less than £500 on clothes, a third spent less than £60 on the supermarket shop and most spend at least an hour a day working on their finances and investments. The simple fact is that you don't get rich by being foolish with your money. What's more, it is remarkably easy to lose your money even if you've been wealthy.

Richard Block, the co-founder of B&Q, currently works at a health food store, having lost the money he'd gained from B&Q in a series of failed business ventures. His partner David Quayle, on the other hand, went on to launch a series of successful ventures and is a millionaire.

can you control your spending?

Think about ways to increase your income.

1 How much does your lifestyle really cost? Count last month's outgoings down to the last penny, from mortgage and bills to money spent eating out, on clothes and at the pub. How does it compare with your income?

2 Take a notebook and jot down for a week every single thing you buy from stamps and beer, to petrol and the supermarket bill. Get your partner to do the same. Then sit down and go through every single item. Was each purchase entirely necessary? Was it worth it, in terms of value or enjoyment? (You may, for instance, decide that a beer with friends was entirely worth it, but that a can bought on the way home and then spilt on the train was not.) Were there any purchases you shouldn't have made? Are there any ways you can reduce spending on your supermarket shopping bill (by buying own brands, for example, instead of well-known names)? If you pare down what you spend to those things that are either essential or add value in terms of enjoyment, how much will you save?

3 Look at your last electricity, gas and water bills. Note down any ways you can reduce the bills this time. Aim to reduce them by at least 5% in the immediate term, more in the medium term.

4 Seen something you want to buy? Take 24 hours before you make a purchase. Do you still really want or need it?

5 Only take out one credit card, and always withdraw a very limited amount of cash.

6 Check your finances regularly. For instance, could you get a better deal on your mortgage? (This might save thousands of pounds.) Your insurance? Your gas, water and electricity providers?

7 Shop around for any major purchase. Do you always pay the asking price? If so, why? Okay, you won't get far haggling in the supermarket over the price of a can of beans. But you may well be able to get a deal by haggling over expensive purchases such as your home, car, home decoration, white goods, hotels, stand-by tickets and car hire. One thing is for sure, if you don't ask for a reduction, it certainly won't be offered.

8 Put aside 10% of your income each week for leisure and pleasure. That's your fun budget to spend, blow and enjoy. By having a clearly defined amount for fun, you are less likely to feel deprived and blow your budget.

9 Note the money you have saved. Put it in a bank or building society account (shop around to find the one with the highest interest rates) while you plan whether to invest it or spend it on a major purchase. (See chapter 5 for more on investment.) Already your new respect for money is helping you think more like a millionaire.

making more of what you've got

Financial security is enormously important to millionaires, second only to having work that is hugely enjoyable. Most set out to do something they enjoyed, but that would also allow them to have the financial security they yearned for.

There is an old saying in business that your best new customers are your existing ones. So before you even start to look at ways to increase your income, a priority should be to look at ways to increase savings and investment on your current income. By making careful decisions you may be able to release substantial capital to start a business (many millionaires have used their savings to fund their initial venture), take further career-related training or even retire earlier. But it's important to have a close look at what you spend. Many people don't realise how much money they regularly outlay. The tips on page 42 should help you with this.

'Anyone who knows the value of a pound and how hard it is to go out and get it won't waste money.'
TOM HARTLEY JUNIOR

The easiest way to increase your income is to make more efficient use of the income you have now

what is your millionaire potential?

Have you got what it takes to make millions? Or are you destined to live life in the slow lane? Take our fun quiz to find out.

1 **Which of these sayings best sums up your attitude to money?**

a) A penny saved is a penny earned.

b) Money is the root of evil.

c) Money can't buy you happiness.

2 **When would you be prepared to negotiate a price?**

a) For all major items – mortgage, car, holiday, hotel, etc.

b) When buying a car.

c) I think haggling is demeaning.

3 **Which of the following do you consciously do to save money?**

a) Save electricity by turning lights off.

b) Never give a tip.

c) Look out for two-for-one offers on own brand, rather than buying full-price, branded products.

4 **Your great aunt Emily dies and leaves you £5,000. What would you use it for?**

a) Investments.

b) The trip of a lifetime.

c) A fabulous, unforgettable party.

5 **If you owned a yacht, would you ...**
a) Spend three months a year on holiday on it, in the South of France?
b) Spend two weeks a year on it and hire it out the rest of the time trying to make a profit?
c) Sell it?

 6 **Where do you prefer to buy your clothes?**
a) Designer boutiques, expensive but worth it.
b) I spend lots of time making my own clothes.
c) Chainstores.

 7 **Which of the following most closely represents your views on work?**
a) It's important to have a work-life balance.
b) I enjoy work.
c) Work is the curse of the drinking classes.

8 **How would you most like to be remembered?**
a) As a success.
b) As a good husband/wife/partner.
c) As a good laugh.

9 **Your firm merges with an Italian firm and you are urged to have closer links. Do you ...**
a) Take a couple of Italian lessons?
b) Do nothing? Everyone speaks English nowadays!
c) Take a crash course in Italy over a long weekend?

10 **How much sleep do you like a night?**

a) I can get by on 6 hours or less.

b) 12 hours.

c) 8 hours.

11 **When you were young which of these would have been your ambition?**

a) To serve society.

b) To win the lottery.

c) To be in control of my own destiny.

12 **You have a tight deadline on a project. Do you ...**

a) Work as long and as hard as necessary to get it just right?

b) Work on it steadily each day, finishing at your normal time?

c) Miss the deadline?

13 **As a child did you ...**

a) Find it easy to concentrate on things you were interested in?

b) Occasionally became diverted?

c) Find it difficult to concentrate and still do?

14 **Which of the following motivates you best?**

a) Praise.

b) Sanctions.

c) Interesting work.

15 **What is your attitude when playing games or sport?**

a) I always try to win.

b) It's not the winning, it's the taking part that counts.

c) I think competition is very unhealthy.

How did you do?

1. a1 b0 c0; 2. a2 b1 c0; 3. a1 b0 c1; 4. a1 b0 c0; 5. a0 b2 c1; 6. a0 b0 c1; 7. a1 b2 c0; 8. a2 b0 c0; 9. a1 b0 c2; 10. a2 b0 c1; 11. a0 b0 c2; 12. a2 b1 c0; 13. a2 b1 c0; 14. a1 b0 c2; 15. a2 b0 c0

Score 16-26: You have got top-dollar millionaire potential. You are careful with your money, have a healthy attitude to it, are hard-working and determined to be successful. Read on to see how you can maximise your potential.

Score 8-16: You have got plenty of millionaire potential, but some way to go if you really want to be seriously rich. Are you prepared to make the sacrifices? Can you be sufficiently dedicated and do you want to be? Can you learn to use money more efficiently? Read on to find out.

Score 0-8: Either you are seriously unhappy at work, a terrible money manager, or an out-and-out sloth. You have plenty of changes in attitude to make if you don't want the pinnacle of your achievement to be reaching for the top shelf in the supermarket! Read on to see how you can sharpen up your act.

2

myths and truths

the vital qualities you need

'If a man has money, it is usually a sign, too,
that he knows how to take care of it;
don't imagine his money is easy to get
simply because he has plenty of it.'

EDGAR WATSON HOWE

It is now time to rid yourself of the preconceptions and mental stumbling blocks that are holding you back from achieving your goals.

Most people are intrigued about the millionaire mind, but convinced they don't have one. Many also have brilliant ideas for start-up businesses which, they are sure, would net them a fortune, but which, alas, they are just too busy to put into action. They may have had incisive ideas about improving services – but which they never got around to doing, only to find that someone else did, to great acclaim, a couple of years later.

All too often it is the things we intended to do, but never got around to doing or lacked the confidence to try, rather than the things we actually did, which we come to regret. Anyone can obtain a millionaire mindset – they just have to believe they can.

Can't is one of the most pernicious words in the English language. It is the belief that we can't that holds most of us back from fulfilling our true potential. One recurring theme of the psychologists interviewed for this book is that so many of us never fulfil our true potential – which is often so much greater than we imagine.

Take, for instance, the classic story of Helen Keller. Born deaf and blind, most people believed she would never learn to read, write or communicate. However, her indefatigable parents and teachers were determined to prove common opinion wrong and Helen Keller went on to achieve all those targets and much more besides, becoming a symbol of both achievement over the odds and sheer bloody-minded tenacity.

It is often the things we planned and didn't do rather than the things we actually did, which we later regret

Most of us lack tenacity. Even worse, we often sabotage our chances by coming up with 'reasons' (really excuses) why we cannot try a certain course or action. Often we argue that if we were to try we would be certain to fail. Great excuses for not applying for promotion, setting ambitious goals or achieving include:

🌀 I could get a better job – but I'm too busy doing this one.

Is every minute really accounted for? How much time do you spend watching TV every week? (The average is 13 hours, not including a further seven hours spent watching while eating and doing other things.) How many hours do you spend socialising or reading the newspaper? Could you sleep an hour less each night for a week, to give yourself time to research what you might want? Are you really, really sure there aren't a few hours in each week that could be better spent advancing your true goals?

🌑 **I'd like to earn more money, but my boss won't pay me more.**
There are a whole host of ways to earn more money. You could apply for promotion, or you could try and earn extra income outside your job (see chapter 3 for more ideas). Even if you were to work a further five hours a week at say £7 an hour (and most people will be able to price their services above this), it amounts to nearly £2,000 a year in extra income.

🌑 **I don't have the right sort of experience for a better job.**
And what makes you think that there is an ideal candidate out there who has all the right qualifications? Some of the millionaires interviewed for this book had applied for positions where they had almost none of the qualifications requested. However, they placed such a strong emphasis on their prior successes that they were offered interviews – and the job.

Even if you don't think your experience is relevant, you could undertake training to make it more so, or research the relevant areas. Thousands of people never get the jobs they yearn for simply because they argue themselves out of applying or decide, bizarrely, that it is safer to stick with the devil they know. In sporting terms, this is the equivalent of not turning up at the starting line. If you want to run, whether it's for the village team or in the Olympics, it's a good idea to turn up to the heats.

After all, the worse that can happen if you do race is that you come last. But last isn't so terrible, as long as you decide it isn't. Failure is only as serious as you make it. In real terms, the worst thing that actually might happen is

If you want to run in a race, it's a good idea to turn up at the starting line

that you waste the cost of a stamp and a few hours writing a CV. However, even writing out your CV is not time wasted: you may well use it for the next job, having learnt what you did wrong in this one. Good salesmen do not give up if they fail to make a sale, they merely move on to the next prospect. Indeed, statistically, the more customers you talk to the more rejections you will receive – but also the more acceptances.

Many people also prevent themselves from even taking the first steps to getting richer simply because they believe that there are a whole range of conditions that rich people automatically fulfil and that they, by circumstances of birth, upbringing or class, simply can't achieve that level of success.

Failure is only as serious as you make it

This is nonsense. Most millionaires did not inherit a millionaire business. A quick glance at *The Sunday Times* Rich List, a guide to the wealthiest people in Britain, shows that there are many hugely successful people who started entirely from scratch.

The following exercise will help you consider ways to change your life.

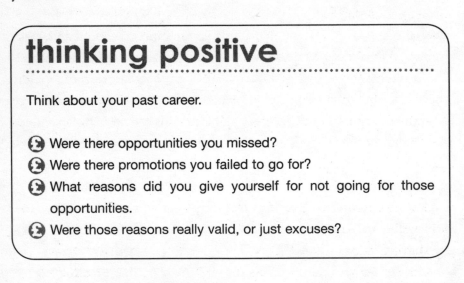

thinking positive

Think about your past career.

- Were there opportunities you missed?
- Were there promotions you failed to go for?
- What reasons did you give yourself for not going for those opportunities.
- Were those reasons really valid, or just excuses?

Below are seven myths that may very well be holding you back – and the reasons why you mustn't allow them to do so.

myths about millionaires that prevent you becoming one

myth one: you have to be born wealthy to become wealthy

Wrong. The Tulip survey shows that a third of British millionaires and multimillionaires come from backgrounds that are distinctly average in terms of income. A quarter of millionaires came from backgrounds where their parents were poor or struggling to survive. Only 2% came from wealthy backgrounds.

A third of the millionaires interviewed for this book are from poor backgrounds. Some, like David Gold, have gone on to be super-rich. Indeed, many of Britain's immigrant millionaires started with nothing. Dame Stephanie Shirley who has earned a multimillion pound fortune through founding the FI Group, now Xansa, arrived in Britain as a refugee from Nazi Germany aged five, with no money and no family. She says that part of her motivation was to prove her life was worth saving.

Of course, you have an easier start in life if you are born into a wealthy family rather than a poor one. And it is certainly easier if you can start a business with money borrowed from mum and dad rather than having to persuade the bank, venture capitalists or everyone who knows you to part with it, but that has nothing to do with the success of the enterprise. When it comes to getting to the top of an organisation wealth may not even buy you a place on the starting ladder.

Only 10% of millionaires feel inheriting money or a business has been a factor in their success

On the other hand, access to capital – finding money from somewhere, anywhere – is crucial to starting a business. However, finding that capital may be down as much to your own tenacity as to your family background. Some of the millionaires featured in this book started with bank loans – though they may have

learn from the millionaires

In an odd way Alexander Amosu, a young black, savvy entrepreneur has trainers to thank for his success. When he went to school wearing a brand his school mates didn't approve of, the ridicule and isolation he suffered made him realise that to be in with the girls as well as the boys, he had to have the right kit. Trouble was, there was no way his family could afford it. He realised that, 'If I wanted something stylish or lavish, I had to get it for myself. I could either steal it or work really hard and achieve it. And I wanted to work for it.'

Alexander started with a paper round and had soon saved enough for the Nike trainers that earned him the acceptability he craved. His awareness of the power of money to change his life meant that he soon graduated to a variety of jobs. He worked part-time in Tandy and Pizza Hut, at one stage doing a shift at one, back-to-back with a shift at the other, in order to save for a car. At 17 he applied for a grant from the Prince's Trust to run a cleaning business, which he ran for three years while he studied. He then moved on to organising events ranging from five-a-side football to enormously popular college club nights. He was always, always working, looking for the next idea to make money.

However, his biggest idea was just around the corner. He discovered that by working various options on his mobile phone, he could introduce ringtones that were different from the standard ones. He sent a few to friends and soon people were queuing to buy them. Indeed, he even challenged someone he'd just met outside a nightclub to a 'battle of the ringtones'. Alexander was so impressed by his new friend's skill at creating ringtones that he invited him to join his new company. Creating customised ringtones was new, different and very exciting.

Alexander admits he had no funding and knew nothing about the application side of producing ringtones, but he was determined to make it happen. 'I know nothing about building a house,' he says. 'But I guarantee that if I wanted to build one, then I'd do the research and I'd know what there was to know. I find out what needs to be done.'

The business took off like a rocket. Within a year of starting the business and aged 25, he had £1 million turnover. More recently he has sold part of the business, while retaining an interest, giving him the chance to move on to the next venture. He knows he will succeed again. 'I tell everyone, motivation plus determination equals success. If you have that no one can stop you.'

had to try several banks – and in one case 15. Others used savings, business angel funding or a variety of combinations. Access to funding is crucial in starting a business, but it is a mistake to think that it is family who normally put up that money.

myth two: you need to be academically brilliant

Great businessmen, top company directors and top managers are brilliant. Brilliant at what they do.

However, that doesn't mean they were academic stars at school or even in the top set. Forty per cent of British millionaires describe their performance at school as distinctly 'average'. Forty-five per cent left school at 18 or earlier (the millionaires over 45 were more likely to have left school early than the younger ones). Many of the millionaires in this book left school at 16 and some even earlier. Often they left with no qualifications. Psychologists point out that while millionaires are certainly not below average intelligence, you do not need to be a genius to become a successful entrepreneur or millionaire! Other qualities, many of which are listed in the 'truths' section of this chapter, are more important.

The British research tallies with research done in the United States by Dr Thomas Stanley, author of *The Millionaire Mind*, which surveyed American millionaires. Dr Stanley discovered that many US millionaires saw themselves as 'the smartest kid in the dumb row'. They did not, by and large, gain straight As at school, nor were they sure-fire certs for the top universities.

There are a variety of theories as to why certain people who later on do so well in life, do so badly at school. One, gaining popularity, is that many successful business people are actually dyslexic. They are incredibly bright, but their technical difficulties with reading and spelling mean they just don't do as well as they should at school. Richard Branson, for instance, is dyslexic, so is US designer Tommy Hilfiger and publisher and former politician Michael Heseltine. Other reasons why people who later become successful in life do badly at school include being too questioning or having a lateral turn of mind, or being full of the sort of energy that makes sitting at a desk for hour after hour, torture. What's more not all schools are equally good and many schools fail to switch on their pupils, whatever their abilities.

This doesn't mean that successful people don't learn lessons at school. They just learn less obvious ones: that you can fail and start again; that failure is largely how you perceive it; that hard work and persistence count; and, above all, that there are other routes to success than the purely academic. Indeed, young entrepreneur Dominic McVey, who made his millions selling scooters and now promotes bands, feels that many people become successful business people because they don't fit in at school and won't fit in easily into employment, either. They are too independent, they don't like taking orders, they want to do things their way and have talents that often aren't fully explored at school.

Millionaires are not generally straight A students

Indeed, Thomas Stanley points out that those with high analytical intelligence – the kids who do best in exams – are often encouraged into extremely competitive areas, such as the law and medicine, with other children who are equally academic. In areas where everyone has to be academic to succeed, only a few can make it to the top. Millionaires, on the other hand, tend to look for niche areas, for more unusual opportunities or even for entirely new areas where they can succeed.

In the real world a host of non-academic qualities matter, from common-sense to a willingness to risk failure

What's more, if at school you are constantly being celebrated for your academic achievement or lauded as 'brilliant' you can develop both arrogance and smugness, a feeling of invincibility and the wrongful idea that the world owes you a living just because you are clever. (You may even turn your nose up at doing those menial jobs which often allow you a real insight into the world of work and which provide a springboard for many business people.)

However, in the real world a whole host of non-academic qualities matter, ranging from common sense to flexibility and a willingness to risk failure – something directly at odds with an academic, qualification-based education.

It may also be that those who have always been successful at school learn to deal with failure much later – and take it much harder. If you have been continually praised for your success, then a small failure, even as small as failing your driving test, can derail you far more easily than those who have had to get used to not being academic superstars.

This is not to rubbish academic qualifications. Many millionaires, such as Sahar Hashemi of Coffee Republic or Karan Bilimoria of Cobra Beer were high-flying professionals before they went into business.

In a world where jobs are increasingly scarce, academic qualifications (or lack of them) are often used as a means of eliminating an initial list of candidates. The professions (law, medicine, teaching, architecture and accountancy) are only open to university graduates. So if you want to become a top professional, your qualifications will be key. However, even if you did badly at school, you can become a mature student and gain the qualifications that will open these doors for you. In academic life motivation and good teaching are critical. You may not have been ready to study at 17 if you couldn't see the point of learning a load of Latin verbs. You may be much more enthusiastic to study at 25 if you want to use your degree in Japanese to trade in Japan.

Most major companies now have graduate training schemes which, to some extent, allow graduates to get a quicker and more in-depth knowledge of the business, than those who have worked for the company since the age of 16. Often these training schemes are used as a fast track. Nevertheless, this does not mean that if you have failed to get on one of these schemes, you are doomed to a life of bean-counting. You can, with perseverance, hard work and flair, overtake the graduates – it may just take you a little more hard work.

The Tulip research showed that nearly 90% of British millionaires had attended either a university or college at some time in their lives. This is often because they wanted to take professional qualifications that would enhance their career. Two-thirds of millionaires in the Tulip survey have some form of professional qualification, though this may well have been obtained as a mature student, in evening classes or part-time at university.

Part-time work can provide you with as many skills as study

If you are 18 now, want to succeed and yet lack a clear direction, it is vital to choose a course that really interests you and that you feel will take you in the direction you need to go. Which university you go to matters less, though clearly in a choice between a degree at a good university and a similar degree at a second-tier one, you should pick the best you can. Do remember, though, that you may learn as much from your holiday jobs and work experience, as from the degree itself.

If you are older, and getting a professional qualification is part of your career-enhancing goals, then sign up for it, even if you do it part-

learn from the millionaires

Tom Hartley Junior is Britain's youngest self-made millionaire (he made his first million at 14, having left school at 11 to attend the 'Hartley University of Life'). He was unhappy at his school and felt the only reason most people attended was to 'kick a football around at breaktime. I was there to learn'.

His father, who had also left school young, took him out and gave him a different education – through the car showroom. He learnt maths by making calculations about sales, geography through the places they delivered cars, current affairs through newspapers and TV, and business studies through the business itself. He even fulfilled the PE requirements of the curriculum by learning to play golf with his dad! (He is now a very accomplished player.)

Tom doesn't feel he missed out by not having a conventional education. Indeed, he feels learning through the business not only made him wealthy but left him better prepared for life than staying on at school would have done. 'I went to school to learn and I didn't feel I was doing a good enough job at learning enough to be in the business I wanted to be in. I left school to learn and what I learnt through the business – and what I am learning – far exceeds any education I could have anywhere in the world.'

time or in the evenings. Interestingly, only 5% of those millionaires who had attended a college or university left before the final years. Self-made millionaires are not quitters.

myth three: you need to have had a stable background

Wrong. While having a stable background and loving parents makes for a happier childhood, the lack of it need not hold you back from

learn from the millionaires

Today David Gold has every luxury a man could have. A huge home with its own grounds, golf course, swimming pool, snooker room and even an airstrip for his own plane. (Gold has a pilot's licence.) Weekends are spent flying up to watch Birmingham City, which David co-owns, taking in the odd day at the races (he owns several race horses), or perhaps choosing a pair of £500 shoes for his extensive wardrobe.

You'd think such immense wealth had to be inherited. You'd be wrong. At one time David was a bricklayer's apprentice and he grew up in grinding poverty in London's East End, enduring a childhood he remembers as 'cold, hungry and very poor'. His mother worked valiantly to sustain her family, selling Christmas garlands at a market, but his father was rarely around.

Early on, David had a big chance. He was talent-spotted playing football, but his father refused to allow him to sign for West Ham and, as a result, the devastated youth had to stick with a bricklaying apprenticeship that he loathed.

He eventually sold his beloved motorbike, his only transport, to buy a small magazine stall with his brother, but a few months later it became clear he was going to run out of money. He recalls visiting the bank manager and asking for a 'monkey' – East End slang for £500. The bank manager didn't understand what he was talking about, nor did David understand the bank manager who told him the loan would be under his 'own cognisance'. But he got the money he needed. (Ironically, years later the bank manager was part of a team of financiers who took him out to lunch.)

Then David had his big break. Staying open late one evening to wait for a lift from his brother Ralph, he noticed that all the top-shelf magazines sold a lot faster after dark. In fact, he'd done better in that one evening than all week. He stayed open late again, sleeping there this time. Soon, the stall was a success and he was working ten or 11 hours a night. He was eventually able to afford two stores which he purchased for £20,000 each and which he sold ten years later for nearly £3 million. The purchaser originally said he'd never pay the £3 million David wanted, so he paid just under!

The diminutive and dapper David Gold feels that, having inched his way up from poverty, there is still the underlying fear of falling back into it. 'There's a fear element attached to your success, the fear that your wealth can be snatched away from you at any moment.'

success in adult life. Nearly 15% of the millionaires in the Tulip survey said they had a difficult or plain unhappy childhood. Interestingly, nearly a quarter of millionaires who were ultrarich (over three million in assets) had had a difficult childhood – suggesting that their circumstances may have given them the drive not only to succeed, but to keep pushing upwards into the ranks of mega success. (The ultrarich had childhood ambitions both to be financially secure and be seen as successful, while 'poorer' millionaires prioritised financial security.) Indeed, some experts believe that many entrepreneurs have had traumatic or difficult episodes between the ages of seven and 14.

Ironically, when the millionaires questioned in the survey by Tulip Research were asked about their level of happiness now, most were either happy or very happy. However, the ones least likely to be content – regardless of their level of wealth – were those who had enjoyed what they described as a 'perfect' childhood'. It seems that if your childhood was idyllic, when it comes to later life, nothing matches up no matter how successful you become. Consolation, perhaps, for all those who didn't have a perfect childhood!

myth four: it's all just luck anyway

Luck plays only a small part in business or career success. Indeed, in the survey of British millionaires, luck was considered only 13th in a list of factors for success, considerably further down than honesty, hard work, intelligence, social skills, having a supportive partner and even being fit. Yes, there may be an

'The harder I practised, the luckier I became.'
GARY PLAYER, GOLF CHAMPION

element of right place, right time, but many people are in the right place at the right time and still fail to act on it. If you look at any company, there will be any number of trainees who have got on to the bottom rung of the ladder, but only a few will make it to the top.

You make your own luck

How many people, for instance, failed to see the success of the dotcoms when they were starting out, but then only joined the boom just as it peaked and crashed? Indeed, Dr Adrian Atkinson points out that entrepreneurs often do not believe luck had much to

do with their success. These are men and women who believe that they control their destiny and who have done so. 'If an entrepreneur were to win the lottery he wouldn't see it as luck,' says Dr Atkinson. 'He would point out that he had bothered to go down to the newsagent and buy the ticket, that he had chosen the numbers and that he had earned the money which bought the ticket in the first place. The fact that the numbers were chosen at random is neither here nor there.' In other words, you make your own luck.

'If you want something badly enough you will get it as long as you are prepared to make goodness knows what sacrifices.' JOHN MADEJSKI

The fact that millionaires are people who have set out on a course and, even if they have had to make a couple of swerves, have got there in the end, suggests that luck plays only a limited role in success.

No one gets to become the chief executive of a major company through luck alone. Even in areas of high unemployment, is it luck when one person is selected for a scarce job over another? Or is it that the person who was chosen is actually better qualified/more able/more enthusiastic/more hard-working or has better references than the other? Bad luck is often used as an excuse for not trying. If you focus, set goals and work hard, it's amazing how much luckier you can become!

myth five: you need to be young to become successful

Success is possible at any age. Indeed, statistically, many more people in their 50s are millionaires than people in their 20s, largely because they have been building their business or career up for the last 20 years.

'As you grow older you need more challenges, not less.'
PRISCILLA CARLUCCIO

However, you can become successful at any age. Antonio Carluccio had a career as a journalist and wine merchant before, aged nearly 40, he started his career in cookery. He and his wife Priscilla had hugely successful careers behind them when they decided to launch their new concept, Carluccio's caffé and delicatessen. 'Not retiring makes us younger,' Antonio explains. 'We work with young people too which keeps us young and it makes us happy. Until we are physically unable, we'll keep doing it.' Priscilla agrees. 'As you grow older you need more challenges, not less.'

Simon Woodroffe, founder of the hugely successful restaurant chain Yo! Sushi and now looking at extending the brand, was nearly 40 when he came up with the idea. Indeed, Richard Prout, a dotcom millionaire, is helping to back a group of entrepreneurs in their 50s and 60s who have all had careers behind them, but have, within the space of a couple of months, managed to raise half a million pounds in backing. Talent, hard work and drive are not the prerogatives of the young.

myth six: you need to have a certain type of personality

Those interviewed for this book have included extremely successful people who are the life and soul of the party and others who are very shy socially, some who are cheerful and flamboyant, others who are contemplative.

You do need to be able to communicate clearly and effectively with customers, suppliers and staff, but this requires you to have a clear vision you can articulate, rather than to be a star turn. Indeed, many entrepreneurs are not good communicators, though good communication is an essential skill for would-be corporate players or professionals.

myth seven: you need to be a crook to get rich

It is, of course, perfectly possible to get rich by robbing a bank (or five), becoming a Mafia godfather, running an international drugs ring or diamond smuggling. However, this is a high-risk strategy that's likely to end up in jail and disgrace. It is one way of getting rich quick – and losing it equally quickly. It is extremely inadvisable.

However, the good news is that the vast majority of millionaires not only see themselves as honest and trustworthy (93%), they also place it number one on their list of attributes that have helped make them a million.

If you are going to buy a used car, would you rather buy it from someone you trust, who has a reputation for customer service and probity, or would you take a chance and buy it for a few quid cheaper from Crooked Joe down the road – hoping that you find him out of prison at the time?

People like to do business with those they trust and respect. If you are offering a customer service, your reputation is critical. This is why people opt to see one GP in preference to their partners, or pick one firm of solicitors instead of another. Yes, price is important in any deal. However, for most people it is not the only consideration.

Not that millionaires are play-it-by-the-book people. They tend to have a hatred of unwieldy, purposeless bureaucracy, red tape and rules that seem to exist for the sake of the rules themselves rather than serving any practical purpose. Many see themselves as rule-breakers. This does not, however, mean that they break the law. Most are canny enough either to find legitimate ways to get around rules that seemed designed to obstruct, or they find advisers who can help discover ways around the problem. If you are worried that your integrity will be compromised by becoming rich, don't be.

will you work your way to success?

1 **Your boss is on holiday. Do you ...**
a) Come in later and leave earlier?
b) Work as normal?
c) Work harder – you want to impress your boss's boss?

2 **You see your dream job advertised. Unfortunately, it asks for five specific skills and you've only got two. Do you ...**
a) Resolve to get at least two more of the skills in the near future so you'll be a contender next time round?
b) Apply for the job anyway, majoring on the skills you've got and ignoring the ones you haven't?
c) Don't apply – what's the point of being rejected again?

3 It is a good friend's birthday party the same evening as you are due to complete a major project. Do you ...

a) Miss the deadline but go to the party? You've got to have a life!

b) Finish the project off and arrive a little late at the party – the best of both worlds?

c) Work late on the project and miss the party? This project really matters.

4 You have gone to a meeting across town, but the client is keeping you waiting. Do you ...

a) Feel cheesed off at their power game?

b) Use the time to phone a friend?

c) Use the time to make work-related calls?

5 If you don't like a job. Do you ...

a) Leave and claim benefit?

b) Leave as soon as you've got another better one or the finance for your own business?

c) Do nothing – all jobs are miserable?

6 You are helping a friend out in their clothes shop. The store closes at 6 p.m. At 5.55 p.m. a woman rushes in, saying she is looking for a dress to wear for a party. Do you ...

a) Tell her you are closing and shut up shop?

b) Tell her you've got nothing in her size?

c) Tell her you've got several in stock and show her?

You work like a millionaire if you answered: c, b, c, c, b, c. The two clearest characteristics of self-made millionaires are that they work hard and that they enjoy work. Work-life balance may be fine for those hoping to be moderately successful. But if you are really ambitious, you'll not only be prepared to put in the hours, you'll be happy to do so.

truths about millionaires

We have now looked at some of the myths about becoming successful and rich. However, both the Tulip survey and research for this book indicate that there are certain values and qualities which the highly successful have in common. Here are the top seven:

millionaires work very hard

This is an understatement. In the vital years of climbing the company ladder or setting up a business, millionaires are prepared to work seven days a week and 18 hours a day! They will cancel a holiday or miss a glittering event if work demands it. They are willing to put in days that end at 2 a.m. when the need requires it. That's because for them work is a passion, their lifestyle as well as their job.

Take Chris Gorman, for instance. In the early days of DX Communications, he worked an 80-100 hour week, but admits it was quite some time before he had anything to show for it. Or the Hartleys, both junior and senior, who have their car showroom in their back garden so that they can be on hand 24 hours a day to make a sale. Or William Frame who used to wake up his workmen at 7 a.m. on a Sunday to get a flat finished if time was running out.

This is because for highly successful people, work is not about time, it's about results. They also really, really enjoy it. There is nothing they like more than talking about their company, career or business, thinking about it and doing what it takes to create that success. Indeed, when it comes to the reasons for their success, millionaires put hard work second only to being trustworthy, with enjoying their work a close third. Taking opportunities and having intelligence, while important, are seen as less crucial.

David Gold recalls how he used to shop at a local store regularly. One day he arrived at 7 p.m. and they shut the door in his face. To him, this reluctance to work overtime, to put in the hours, symbolised the fact that the shopkeeper would never 'get to the next rung of the ladder'. He is right. If you want to be a success, you aren't going to be able to work nine to five – until you are already successful.

Not that life is a continual slog for millionaires. For most of them the hardest years were establishing the business (though for company high-flyers, the hardest working years may be at the end of their career when they are at their most senior).

> *'My parents taught me that if you put your head down, worked hard and persisted, you could achieve anything.'*
> SAHAR HASHEMI

As the business grows, some (though not all) work less or cherry-pick particular areas. Some even sell out and retire to the golf course, though many find they cannot retire for too long!

> **For successful people work isn't just about time. It's about getting results**

The Tulip survey reveals that, on average, millionaires work 55 hours a week, with multimillionaires working an average of 64 hours per week. Multimillionaires are also more likely to work on holiday, generally because they are running their own business and businesses. (Interestingly, in general the self-employed, whether small scale or mega-successful, are happier than the employed, probably because they have more control over their own destiny.)

they are time aware

The mobile phone has been a boon for productive people. No more sitting on a train, unable to work, no more having to spend five unproductive minutes hanging out. As a group, the millionaires interviewed have been the most time-conscious group of people I have ever come across. One lamented the fact I'd arrived ten minutes early for an interview. Another's secretary gave me a down-to-the-minute explanation of when her boss would arrive. A couple tried to eat lunch, talk

> # learn from the millionaires
>
> **Julie Hester, a former policewoman, was a stay-at-home mum with four children when a solicitor friend confided how difficult it was to get property searches through. Julie realised it was just a question of accessing the public records, rather than waiting for the local authority to do the searches, and volunteered to help out. The service was so useful that the solicitor recommended her to other solicitors and the business began to blossom.**
>
> 'I'd thought it was going to be a part-time job,' says Julie, 'but the hours just kept increasing.' Eventually Julie was getting up at 6 a.m. to prepare reports, then getting her children up and seeing them off to school, before starting to work again. After school, she looked after her children until bedtime and then worked again until 10 p.m., 11 p.m., midnight. This hugely strenuous schedule was exhausting – and vital in getting the business off to a flying start. Within six months of setting up Julie had earned £60,000 which encouraged her husband Gary to leave his own job and join the company.

and use the phone at the same time. (It's not easy, but it can be done!) Successful people are to time-efficiency what texting is to teenagers. This is because they realise that time is a commodity – but one we cannot increase.

They are therefore extremely ruthless with their time, continually prioritising and allotting time only to those activities they consider worthwhile or enjoyable. They are happy to use time for things they value. The Tulip survey showed that they average over 12 hours a week for leisure and have four holidays a year – but they resent spending time on things they do not want to spend time on. They are not good queuers or the sort of people likely to sit quietly and not make a fuss if the first course takes an hour to be served. They are impatient to get things done and prefer action to inaction. It's important to them to get things done and to get them done fast.

they need to achieve

The people in this book are success stories. To them success, particularly their own definition of it, is crucial. They see themselves as successful and they generally wanted to be successful from a very young age. Nearly all describe themselves as ambitious individuals. According to the Tulip survey, the most popular definition of success for those owning their own business is, not surprisingly, financial security. Many millionaires see financial security as almost synonymous with freedom and control over their own destiny. The second most popular millionaire ambition in the Tulip survey was to work at something they enjoyed, but this was more popular with corporate high-flyers than business people. Women were more likely to prioritise enjoyment over money.

It seems that while many millionaires can afford to retire early, few would choose to, simply because this would not chime with their definition of success: working in something they enjoy and being financially successful. Indeed, several said they had made attempts to slow down, but had become bored and frustrated and were happy to get back into the swing of business life. Basically, those who value achievement most are those who are prepared to work hardest at getting it.

Being in a job you loathe uses up energy faster than the national grid. Doing a job you love gives you more

they have energy

There are no dozy millionaires. You don't get to the top by sleepwalking. All of the millionaires, whether running their own business or top professionals, have enormous energy. About half had played sport to a high level in their youth. Many continued to play or were frequent visitors to the gym. Others, like Chris Gorman, can get by on very little sleep. His energy is palpable and extremely useful both in getting through an enormous workload and motivating his team.

That doesn't mean you have to be an ex-Olympian to stand a chance of becoming wealthy (though it is amazing how many sports-people start a successful new venture once their sports career is over). Doing something you enjoy that utilises your skills and talents promotes energy. If you are doing something you love, something you believe in and something that you know will ultimately make you richer, it's amazing how time flies and how little it will feel like work. Being in a job you loathe uses up energy faster than the national grid. Doing a job you love can give you more!

they focus

Millionaires keep their goals and ambitions firmly in mind. They are single-minded, able to concentrate for long periods on the things that interest them and they are not interested in, or influenced or diverted by anything they perceive as being irrelevant to what they are trying to achieve.

Mega-successful people are focused on the achievements they want for themselves, whether that is running the most profitable widget business in town, becoming the number one producer of measuring equipment, or becoming chief executive of a major company. What they have in spades is concentration, goals, targets and milestones. They are not the sort of people to get blown off course.

All successful people are highly motivated, but the source of that motivation does differ as to whether you are naturally entrepreneurial, or more of a company person or professional. Entrepreneurial types are entirely self-driven with their own definition of success. Corporate and professional types tend to need more recognition and approval from both society in general and their peers in particular. Put bluntly, they need more appreciation of the sort that comes from leading and being part of a team.

they are hugely competitive

One of the most revealing aspects of the millionaire mind could be seen when the television series *Mind of a Millionaire* held a day of tests to assess whether there was indeed a millionaire personality. A group of 15 self-made millionaire entrepreneurs were invited to mix incognito with a group of 15 ordinary citizens. They then took part in various tests and competitions to see if the psychologists could determine who was a successful entrepreneur or millionaire and who wasn't.

One of the most clearly distinguishing factors that emerged early on was that the millionaires were far more competitive than the normal citizen. They argued with the referee, they played to win, a few even cheated. Whatever the task, even when it was seemingly pointless, they needed to win. And they made no secret of their pique if they lost. The non-millionaires, on the other hand, took the

learn from the millionaires

Richard Prout makes Michael Schumacher look as if he is trundling along in the bus lane. When Richard isn't putting his limitless energy into work, moving his sleeping bag into the office to make sure the job gets done, then he's literally jumping off a mountain for fun.

Richard is a fanatical paraglider and has flung himself off peaks all over the world. (He can even be winched up from his home and has bought a mountain in New Zealand to fly off!) If he fancies a more humdrum sort of day, then he might just mountain-bike up to the peak instead, or ski down it. That's if he's not motor-racing. Frenetic and driven, he literally 'eats life at a hundred miles an hour'. It is this huge activity and energy that enabled him to start SmartGroups.com so quickly – and then sell it for £60 million all within a year. Life in the fastest of fast lanes, indeed.

competitions in a much more light-hearted manner, saying such things as 'it's just a bit of fun', or 'it's the taking part that counts', or even 'none of this really matters'.

This element is vital to success in competitive areas. You can be an excellent social worker, without having to compete with other excellent social workers. On the other hand, if you want to create a top brand, be a top salesperson, make your company the top in its field or the most profitable, or both, you have to play to win.

'I don't believe in this "it's the taking part not the winning that counts". To me that's a loser speaking. There are winners and there are losers. You are either one or the other.' TOM HARTLEY SENIOR

That is not to say that successful people compete in every area of their lives. Few of them are likely to, say, attempt to win prizes for DIY. What they do is choose arenas they feel they can do well in and then compete like crazy.

The competitive element is vital to success as a millionaire

David Gold, for instance, owns several racehorses but rarely bets on any of them. He feels that in a field of 17 horses, his chances of winning are considerably lower than betting on a football game where there is a one-in-three chance of winning and a two-in-three chance of not losing – considerably better odds.

they learn from the best

Many of the myths that surround millionaires – that they were all rich to start with, or that they've just had luck on their side – emanate largely from envy. However, many of the millionaires interviewed had a different approach. Early on in their careers or business life, they had seen someone whom they had admired or a business they felt was well run, and they had taken the opportunity to learn. Sometimes the person they learnt from was not particularly pleasant or, indeed, even willing to act as a mentor, but they had watched and observed all the same. One millionaire told me that his personal mentor was curmudgeonly and difficult, but he was a fantastic problem-solver, and the young businessman was able to learn from that.

Similarly, you can learn a great deal by taking a low-paid job in an industry that you are interested in – just to be sure that it really is what you want to do. Becoming a waiter will teach you more about catering than eating out will. It is often, interestingly, those who have been at the sharp end of the NHS, such as former nurses, who make the best managers, not those who had management training in other areas.

exercise: what you need to learn

Think about the qualities of successful millionaires. Which of these do you have already? Which do you need to learn or improve?

entrepreneurial flair

Not all millionaires are entrepreneurs. You can become a millionaire by gaining a very senior post in a company, by becoming a top-flight professional or even by being right at the top of the public service tree. Becoming a successful actor, musician, sportsperson, or a celebrity, famed for being famed, are other routes.

However, entrepreneurs do have certain distingushing characteristics and it is interesting just how many of them started an entrepreneurial career when they were, literally, kids. Here are just a few of the entrepreneurial school activities undertaken by the millionaires featured in this book:

David Quayle is a serial entrepreneur best known for his co-founding of the DIY chain, B&Q. (He's the Q.) David started his retail career at the tender age of seven. His father was in the RAF, stationed in Germany after World War Two. While there, David noticed that the American pencils in the NAAFI (airforce recreational centre) were far more attractive than their leaden, dull, wartime English counterparts. He bought a stack for a penny each and sold them in school in England for fourpence – a profit of 300%! (Even the canniest retailer rarely achieves this.)

By 11 he was dealing in sweet coupons. (Sweets were still being rationed in the early fifties.) He'd buy sweet coupons from those fortunate enough not to have a sweet tooth and sell them on when they were date-ready.

'Persuading people to buy something is like fishing,' says David. 'No one goes fishing because they haven't got enough to eat. You enjoy casting the bait and waiting to see if it's taken. It's the thrill of the chase, the hunt. Retailing gives me the same sort of buzz!'

Tom Hartley Senior made his first car sale at 11 when he overheard a friend of his father's, a William Barton, express disappointment in a new Range Rover that he had just bought. Coincidentally, another friend of his father's said how much he liked the same model. Tom set up a deal between them and earned £250 for his acumen, a good sum in those days. He soon realised he had a talent for the business, so that by 15 he was touring the country in his own chauffeur-driven car, finding cars at auction to buy and sell on.

Chris Gorman's first entrepreneurial venture started when he became a newspaper boy. He noticed that the newsagent was often stressed out, trying to organise the deliveries and establish which papers went where. Chris offered to take the job off his hands, and do it within the same budget, taking any profit for himself. Not only was he able to run the round, he was able to do so for £40, netting himself £10 profit and, for most of the time, able to stay in the warm shop, rather than out on a cold bike. The only downside, he recalls, was that when a paper boy didn't turn up he had to do their round himself *and* organise the papers.

Some entrepreneurs find the field they want to work in very quickly. Richard Prout, dotcom millionaire, loved computers from a young age. A neighbour worked for Intel Corporation who were having an open day for the close relatives of staff. The neighbour's son wasn't remotely interested in computers so she sneaked Richard in, telling him to claim he was her offspring. Richard found himself standing next to 'some fat guy who wasn't in a suit', next to a large schematic of the 8080 chip, then the latest word in technology. The man asked if he knew what it was and what he thought about it. Richard said it was rubbish. This could have been unfortunate as the man turned out to be the inventor of the chip. However, he was so impressed by Richard's knowledge of computers and by his chutzpah, that he offered him a holiday job.

are you a budding entrepreneur or a corporate whizz kid?

Everyone wants to succeed, but often success is just as much about finding the right environment as our innate abilities. So how do you decide if your strengths lie in running your own business, climbing the corporate ladder, or in professional or adminstrative roles such as the civil service? Take Dr Adrian Atkinson's questionnaire to find out where to concentrate your energies.

instructions

This questionnaire is made up of statements representing things that people consider to be important to their way of life and business. These statements are grouped into sets of three.

The situation you are asked to imagine yourself in is that you are thinking of starting your own business. Examine each set of three statements. Within each set, find the **one statement** of the three which represents what you consider to be the **most important** to you in the context of starting your own business.

Example:

> a) Be clear about your life goals. ✓
> b) Use decision techniques to solve problems.
> c) Ensure that you know what is expected of you.

© Human Factors (UK) Ltd

In some cases it may be difficult to decide which statement to mark. Make the best decision that you can. This is not a test; there are no right or wrong answers.

If you were starting your own business which of the following would you see as most important:

1
a) Be willing to work long hours.
b) Try to develop many different products/services at one time.
c) Get the products/services offered perfect before getting sales.

2
a) Understand the way your customers think.
b) Surround yourself with people you can trust.
c) Not start the business without all the finance required.

3
a) See work as relaxation.
b) Keep your existing job till your start-up is well established.
c) When you meet a business obstacle, realise that many cannot be overcome.

4
a) Be willing to sacrifice family life to move the business forward.
b) Get a degree before starting up your own business.
c) Make sure you have a good pension before starting up your own business.

5
a) Raise money by selling your home and car.
b) Seek out experienced people for advice.
c) Try hard to be seen as a reasonable person.

© Human Factors (UK) Ltd

6
a) Luck plays little part in a business becoming successful.
b) Need to spend money to make money.
c) Take your time to make all important decisions.

7
a) People who perform badly should be fired.
b) Be careful to let others win arguments.
c) When a decision is made do not change it the next day.

8
a) Know each week how your cash flow is for the next six weeks.
b) When hiring someone, first impressions are all important.
c) Always involve colleagues in making decisions.

9
a) Treat others as you would treat yourself.
b) Start only when you completely understand your market.
c) Be willing to overlook your employees' mistakes.

10
a) Keep chasing every hot prospect till they say yes or no.
b) Try to make as much money as quickly as possible.
c) Realise that customers are often wrong.

11
a) Customers are worth listening to.
b) Important for you to have a big office to impress your clients.
c) Make sure you get home to your family by 7 p.m. and don't work on the weekend.

12
a) Do not diversify – stick to what you know.
b) Never overstretch your resources.
c) Only aim for the highest quality.

Marking

Mostly As – Entrepreneurial: You have lots of entrepreneurial potential for starting your own business and making it highly successful. You work hard, are prepared to devote all your energies to a business you believe in and understand that the business comes first. And you are a risk-taker too, all ingredients for making a success of developing your own business!

Mostly Bs – Corporate: You show the potential for building a business. However, you are likely to prefer to carry this out within a structured, organisational context. You prefer to have like-minded colleagues to work with and who can help you to develop ideas. You probably rely on the organisational structure to give you support from other functions such as sales and marketing.

Mostly Cs – Professional/administrative: You are likely to value doing things properly in an organised and structured way. You may value professional expertise and are unlikely to become involved in enterprises unless you feel well qualified to add value through your expertise. You are prepared to work hard but also value quality of life. You prefer a balance between work and leisure. You are probably cautious about taking risks and may prefer the tried and trusted route to the more risky route.

making it

getting to that first million

*'Whenever you see a successful business,
someone once made a courageous decision.'*
PETER DRUCKER

Essentially there are two realistic ways of making your fortune. The first is climbing the ladder whether in a company, professional practice or public service (though public service tycoons are few and far between). The second is to become an entrepreneur and to start and run your own business. To some extent, which way you choose will have been determined by your answers to the quizzes in the previous chapters. However, certain entrepreneurial qualities, such as thinking out of the box and persistence, are also valued by corporations. As entrepreneurs have so much to teach us about wealth creation it is well worth exploring their skills and aptitudes.

Indeed, it is fascinating how much entrepreneurs have in common with each other. As mentioned earlier, for part of the programme

how good are you at scenting opportunities?

1 **If you suffer a product or service that is bad do you think...?**
a) That's just the way life is.
b) Someone should do something about that.
c) I bet there's a way of doing that better – let's think about it.

2 **Do you believe that in life luck accounts for:**
a) 90% of your destiny.
b) 70% of your destiny.
c) 50% or less of your destiny.

3 **If you go to a corporate event do you...**
a) Give your business card to anyone who may be relevant to you?
b) Give it only if someone makes a point of asking?
c) You don't have a business card and if you did you'd forget to take it?

4 **A colleague lets slip that a job you'd like to get is about to become vacant. Do you...**
a) Find out who the relevant person is to talk to and arrange to talk to them informally?
b) Wait until the job is advertised?
c) You don't apply for the job – you never get anything decent?

5 **Your office is moving to an industrial desert. There is not even a coffee bar there. What do you do?**
a) Nothing.
b) Lobby management for a canteen.
c) Start assessing the demand from your colleagues for a sandwich service – maybe there's a niche here.

(Solutions on page 122)

Mind of a Millionaire, Optomen, the TV production company behind the series, took a group of millionaire entrepreneurs and matched them like-for-like with a group of ordinary citizens, then sent them on an away-day together.

The citizens and millionaires were all anonymous and instructed to dress down to avoid possible recognition. The group was then put through a series of tests and problem-solving exercises. Psychologists from Human Factors International were asked to spot which were entrepreneurs and which were not, judging by their values and reactions. The psychologists had a success rate of well over 80%, suggesting that there are huge similarities in the mindsets of successful business people. So what are they and can you learn them?

finding the right opportunities

In order to start a business, you first need to come up with an idea for a business, preferably one that fills a gap in the market. There is no point being the 33rd pizza parlour on the high street. The good news is that remarkably few entrepreneurs come up with a totally new product, although there are some. Mandy Haberman, for instance, invented the Anywayup Cup, a spill-proof toddler cup that has revolutionised the toddler feeding market. However, she and giants such as James Dyson are actually inventor-entrepreneurs, a relatively rare breed. What most entrepreneurs do is see a pattern that no one else does, a gap in the market, a more efficient way of doing things, or a better way to deliver a product. For instance, Britain has the most competitive beer market in the world with imports from as far afield as Australia and the US. There is also plenty of high-quality real ale and a vibrant market in other alcoholic drinks.

'Most people go through life with their eyes shut, accepting the status quo rather than thinking if only there could be this or that. But I feel anything is possible – things can always be improved.' MANDY HABERMAN

learn from the millionaires

When Basil Newby comes home from a hard day's work on the night shift, he likes to listen to the birdsong, or watch the peacocks at his spectacular, ivy-encrusted country home, or even to tend the miniature Falabella horses he breeds as relaxation. But then perhaps it's not surprising Basil appreciates peace and quiet when he's at home with his longterm partner.

His working life is noisy, full of light, sound and people as he flits between the clubs he owns in Blackpool (often called Basil-Pool because he is so well-known), gossiping, bantering and overseeing. Indeed, he's never been to bed before 3 a.m. on a working night!

But when he started his first club, he was a complete unknown. Starting a new club when you are unknown (and the town already has many successful ones) might seem like trying to set up a cosmetic surgery clinic in Hollywood. However, when Basil set up his first club, The Flamingo, back in 1979, he was convinced there was a gap in the market. 'There were clubs, but they weren't very good,' he says. 'I did my research and they didn't have entertainment, or a cheap drinks night. I looked for what they weren't supplying – and supplied it.' (Ironically, Basil is a teetotaller.)

Shortly after opening, having established there was only one tiny gay bar in town which closed at 10.30 p.m. just as the rest of the town was hotting up, he decided to make The Flamingo a gay club. He has never looked back. In the first six months he upped his turnover on a Saturday night nearly 400%. However, there were plenty of problems. One night the boiler packed in and various firms of plumbers refused to come out because they claimed they were scared of catching AIDS. 'So we just had to keep on ringing 'round,' he laughs. While others might have panicked, his laid-back attitude has helped him keep expanding in a very competitive world.

Basil's philosophy was to look for what was not being done well – the gap in the market – and make sure his clubs did it better. 'I'm very particular,' he says. 'For instance, all my managers know that I go absolutely mad if there's a light bulb not working. I wouldn't like it if I'd paid to go into a club and the light wasn't working, so why should they?' His flagship venue is now Funny Girls, a transvestite revue and bar, which attracts both straight and gay customers.

Basil had seen similar concepts in Thailand and Canada, but he admits that when he decided it could be adapted for the Blackpool market, even his partner was sceptical. 'But I felt I had to do it; it was all there in my head.'

Basil believes that once you have found your gap in the market, you need to have a clear vision of what you want to achieve, a mental picture of how your product will be when it's complete. This is what he aims for with all his venues, and he doesn't rest until the reality matches up.

When Karan Bilimoria came up with the idea for Cobra Beer, looked at in the context of a literally overflowing market, he might have seemed crazy. What he had spotted, though, was that there was a gap in the market for a certain type of beer: one that would go specifically with Indian cuisine, which was less gassy than other beers. Similarly, there is nothing gobsmackingly radical about opening a coffee shop. Coffee shops have been prominent in British cultural life since Samuel Johnson and his mates used to gather for gossip, coffee and snuff in the 17th century.

What Sahar Hashemi and her brother Bobby spotted was that there was a gap in the market for the sort of clean-cut coffee houses serving a range of exotic coffees and the fat-free muffins that Sahar had enjoyed when she had lived in the US: a lifestyle coffee shop, if you like. The result was Coffee Republic, now a household name.

People bought and sold cars privately before *AutoTrader*, they just had to do so without the benefits of colour photography and slick presentation that John Madejski introduced. Hobbyists like to chat to each other, online or off. Richard Prout realised there was an opportunity to create tailor-made websites for hobbyists that would act as a magnet for advertisers in those markets. By creating the high-quality SmartGroups.com, he was able to develop a product that would sell for £60 million within a year of starting up.

What most entrepreneurs do is see a pattern that no one else does, a gap in the market

All these ideas exploited gaps in the market – and filled them. However, that doesn't mean it's first time lucky. Many entrepreneurs have several start-up attempts before coming up with the business that is a big success. It's back to the old maxim, try, try, try and try again. You might succeed with your first idea, but if not you need to be prepared to go back to the drawing board and start again if it doesn't work. Interestingly, multi-millionaires were more likely than those with lesser amounts to see grabbing opportunity as vital to success.

finding your own gap in the market

How do you go about finding an idea for the product or service that will make you rich?

Essentially, it's very simple; you need to be your own customer. Think about products and services that you have used that aren't as good as they could be, or where there is a distinct lack. Be realistic, we all know that the train service is poor, but you are unlikely to win the franchise unless you are already rich and powerful (and would you want to?) On the other hand, you might think about the sort of services that would improve

You need to be enthused by and knowledgeable about the product or service you offer

learn from the millionaires

Creativity is very important to David Quayle. There is nothing he likes better than to have an idea and make it work, whether it's creating a major business like B&Q, painting in his own studio (his big indulgence), or currently commissioning a musical about the life of Lord Nelson.

It might seem a jump from selling pots of paint to funding a musical, but essentially David is excellent at spotting the opportunity to create something. When working in Belgium he was intrigued by the presence of hypermarkets situated on the outskirts of town. In Britain, there was nothing like this and he was interested to note that they all had DIY departments where the customers picked the items for themselves rather than being served. A few months later, back in Britain, his employers were experimenting with a new concept of DIY store. David was invited to view it and was horrified. 'I realised that absolutely everything about it was wrong. They had men in white coats serving and weighing out every nail for the customer and measuring every metre of flex. I knew that wasn't the way to go about it.'

Using the hypermarket model, he began to look for sites big enough for the warehouse-type store he imagined. He finally found one in Southampton. Finance came through a variety of sources, including a bank guarantee from his then wife. 'I took a £12,000 overdraft but we were careful with buying our stock. If a supplier said they supplied something in dozens, we'd ask them to split a packet.' He ensured that although there were, for example, several cans of white paint on the shelf, there was only one of each colour, so he wouldn't be left with stacks of unsold paint. As a result the initial outlay of stock cost only £7,000, leaving money in the bank to buy more of the fast-selling items. When B&Q opened it was an instant success. That's because although they sold essentially the same products as any other hardware shop, they sold them in a way the customer wanted to buy.

train travel. There are, for instance, several businesses making a healthy living out of forecourt snack and coffee bars. Are there other gaps? Better cleaning services, for instance, or value-added possibilities?

You will find that your best ideas come from those areas you know about and care about the most. Remember, you need to be enthused by the product or service you offer and to become intensely knowledgeable about it. There may be a market in better bridge building, but if you know zero about engineering, you may not be the best person to solve problems in this area. Look for patterns too – things that could go together.

> '**There is a buzz about creating something successful where there was nothing before.**' DAVID QUAYLE

Julie Hester was friendly with a solicitor who mentioned how frustrated he was by the difficulties of getting a land registry search back from the local authority quickly. Julie realised that by far the most efficient way to perform the search was to go down to the local authority and look up the information, rather than waiting for the various departments to check out their particular piece of the jigsaw. By finding a quick way of accessing information that was available, she was able to cut through the hold-ups – and build her business, the Property Search Group, which has now been successfully franchised throughout the UK.

> **You need to be your own customer**

When you have an idea that seems, to you, to work, research it thoroughly. This is vital because you may discover people are not as interested as you think in your product, or that they aren't prepared to pay a realistic price for it, or there is already a thriving business in it that is shortly coming to your area.

Remember that different sectors have different demands. You may be able to start a dotcom relatively cheaply and become successful within a year. It can take a little longer to become established in 'bricks and mortar' retailing. However, it generally takes between eight and

exercise: finding opportunities

A To help find your own gap in the market, ask yourself:

1 What services do I use that aren't good enough? Is there a way I can make them better using my skills and knowledge?

2 What products do I use that could be improved? How could I improve them? (See Dr Atkinson's brainteasers on page 103 for ways to improve your problem-solving ability.)

3 Is there a gap in the retail market that I could fill? (Use your life experience to guide you in this one. Great businesses have been started from frustration at being unable to buy a big enough bra, to discovering you could make different signature rings on a mobile phone from those offered as standard.)

4 What is the market doing at the moment? Which sectors, products and markets are expanding, which are contracting?

5 Do I have an interest that can help guide me in my search for a better product or service?

B If you come up with a humdinger of an idea – and remember it probably won't happen overnight – the next stage is to ask yourself:

1 Do I care enough about this to be willing to work on it night and day for the next five or ten years? If not, is this just a sideline? (See page 110.)

2 Does this idea really matter? Will customers be willing to pay a realistic price for it?

3 Am I willing to spend a great deal of time and effort researching this product or service? If not, how can this really be the right product or service for me or anyone else?

ten years to get a science-based project off the ground, as venture capital is often required and the venture capitalists expect to see a management team in place.

an independent outlook

Once you have a good idea, you need to research its viability thoroughly. You will need to enter whole new worlds of suppliers, pricing, market research and marketing. However, even if your research confirms your greatest hopes, do not expect others to share your enthusiasm, even your nearest and dearest. When Karan Bilimoria decided to create Cobra Beer, his parents worried that he would come unstuck, and felt he should take up a profession. He admits that if a management consultancy had run a feasibility study, they would probably have rejected the idea. However, Karan researched the beers available, knew there was a gap in the market and was convinced he could fill it. When Robert Braithwaite decided to build British motorboats, his own father did not rate his son's chances of success. It was Robert's father's business partner who put up cash to start the fledgling business.

According to psychologist Dr Adrian Atkinson, one of the common traits of entrepreneurs is that they have a low need for affiliation. What this means is that they are less desperate for the approval or admiration of their peers or friends than the rest of us. They are content with their own company, don't need to be loved or approved of by everyone and are truly self-motivated, rather than motivated by the praise and approval of others. Indeed, the Tulip survey found that half of those owning their own business say that it doesn't bother them if others around them disapprove of what they do. This contrasts with less

> '**The day you say you've made it is the day you are finished. I'm always trying to make a better product.**' ROBERT BRAITHWAITE

than a third of professionals and company directors. Overall two-thirds of those who owned their own businesses felt that there was an element of this in their personality. What's more, over a quarter of business owners felt that others might perceive them as arrogant or abrasive. The richer the person, the more likely they were to see themselves as self-reliant, enthusiastic and dedicated to success. Self-image is, in many ways, a self-fulfilling prophecy.

Entrepreneurs aren't motivated by the praise of others

This disregard for the good opinion of others can be crucial to success, particularly when you are starting a business. Time and time again, the business people interviewed told stories of how others had greeted their idea with scepticism, doubted their ability to get it off the ground or had a positively gloomy prognosis of their chances of success.

What's more, creating business, as an activity, isn't necessarily prestigious – at least until it is successful. There may be a very comfortable living to be made in inventing a device that removes bird dirt swiftly from buildings or surfaces, or in establishing a pest control company, but that doesn't mean it is considered exciting!

Entrepreneurs have no fear of being alone or different

To be an entrepreneur it is often crucial to be able to stand alone, stand out from the crowd and question the accepted wisdom.

Events at the problem-solving day organised for the programme *Mind of a Millionaire* confirmed this view. Entrepreneurial types often stood back from activities they did not relate to and they were happy to spend time being solitary. This lack of need for validation from others is crucial when it comes to deciding whether to follow a business idea. Basically, if you are convinced that your idea is right, you need to develop a thick skin when it comes to other people's views of what you should or should not be doing. This is where your self-belief really shows.

enthusiasm counts

Enthusiasm and optimism are vital to an entrepreneur. After all, if you are lackadaisical or unethused by your product, why should anyone else be remotely excited? In the early days, your enthusiasm is often the only tangible asset the business has to offer. A new entrepreneur generally has no track record, no credibility, and shoestring funding. It is enthusiasm that can attract both funding and customers. Often entrepreneurs told me how it was their enthusiasm for, and their passionate belief in, the business that persuaded the bank manager to

learn from the millionaires

It's hard to persist in the face of disapproval or incredulity from your colleagues or friends, but even harder when it's your father who is sure you are making a mistake.

Yet, that's what Alexander Amosu came up against when he decided to launch RnB Ringtones. At the time, he was a student on a sound engineering course at university, and his father urged him to put off his idea of leaving the course to start a business. He felt that Alexander could play with ringtones in his spare time, but that he should stick with his qualification, not risk his degree for a speculative business.

Alexander knew his father's advice was sensible, but he also knew it was wrong for him. 'If I hadn't believed in myself I would have followed his advice, 'cos it's hard when it's your father talking. We had arguments about it. But I knew that I had to make my own choices and that if I did make a mistake, then I'd learn from it. I have to have control over my own life: sometimes I may be right, sometimes I may make mistakes, but it has to be me who makes the decisions for me.'

give them their first loan, the customers to give them a try-out or their suppliers to agree at least to talk to them. In the place of an established track record, enthusiasm is often your only and most persuasive weapon.

Indeed, in the Tulip survey entrepreneurs were far more likely to describe themselves as enthusiastic and impulsive than either professionals, company directors or those working in the public service.

Enthusiasm is often your only persuasive weapon

going for risk

Successful entrepreneurs are risk-takers. In the Tulip survey, the business people's willingness to take risks distinguished them from the corporate players who were a little more cautious, from the professionals who were more cautious again and particularly from those working in the public sector who were ultra-cautious. That is because business is a high-risk and high-reward game. Get it right and you could earn yourself a million, three million, 60 million. Get it wrong and you could end up losing everything from your career to your home. Often entrepreneurs take risks that make the more cautious feel dizzy just at the prospect. It is this risk-taking that is vital to the millionaire mindset and potential.

So why do they do it? Entrepreneurs are nature's optimists. When starting out, they perceive their chances of success as being high, even if others might rate them lower. They believe that not only can they succeed, but they *will* succeed, and they are willing to put in the effort to do so. They are not worriers or fretters. While several admitted to the odd sleepless night where a risk looked like it might not come off, for the most part they are able to take risks without dwelling on the possible negative consequences, or fretting about what would happen if it all went wrong. For them, what

Entrepreneurs are nature's optimists

looks like an unacceptable risk to others is actually one that they have shrewdly calculated should come off.

Indeed, one of the reasons they do not fret is that they perceive their chances of winning as very high. Tom Hartley Senior admits that buying a stock of expensive cars means he is regularly carrying stock worth £5 million. However, he believes that he can sell those cars and make a profit, so he does not worry about the debt he has incurred.

During the *Mind of a Millionaire* exercises to discover who was an entrepreneur, the millionaires consistently took more risks than the normal citizens. Indeed, in one particular game, each team was asked to throw a ball at a net, from a distance that varied from 1 to 20 metres. Naturally, the further back you stand, the greater the risk of missing. If you hit the ball into the net you scored the number of metres that you had tried from. If you failed, you were minus to the same number of metres. The psychologists watching the exercise were looking for people who aimed high, and weren't worried about failing. Entrepreneurs consistently tried to score the ball from further away, in one case from twenty metres at each throw. Some took highly calculated risks, for instance scoring two balls close up and then standing well back for the third in an all-or-nothing final fling strategy. Indeed, even among entrepreneurs there are those who will take larger risks and those who calculate extremely carefully. David Quayle, for instance, says he takes risks, but those risks are highly calculated: 'I wouldn't risk the shirt off my back or my life,' he says.

For most entrepreneurs the highest risk occurs when the business is just starting. This is when they may need to offer their house as guarantee, take large

> '*Without the risk there would be no reward and no thrill.*'
> TOM HARTLEY SENIOR

loans or use savings they can ill-afford to lose. However, at the same time, this is also paradoxically when they have the least to lose as they are not yet established or successful. Most highly successful businesses start as shoestring operations, with the owner often prepared to take

learn from the millionaires

Basil Newby feels that his enthusiasm helped pull his business through in the early months, when a series of unfortunate events meant it almost went under.

Basil had been running the Flamingo Club for six months and was making a real impact on the Blackpool scene, when disaster struck. Basil's landlord, the leaseholder, became bankrupt and it looked like Basil would lose his venue. In desperation, he visited the owner of the building, an old lady. 'I was so enthusiastic that she said that if I could raise the money, she'd let me have the whole building for £100,000.' Basil then set about persuading breweries to advance the money. Most listened – until he told them the Flamingo was a gay club – at which point they said that they simply didn't do business 'with clubs like those'. Eventually, Basil found a brewery wanting to move into Blackpool. He met the representative and his enthusiasm was so contagious that not only did the brewery put up the money, they did so on an interest-free basis. Basil feels that his enthusiasm for his club, and the fact that he'd already increased turnover, really helped persuade people to give him a chance, just at the point when it looked like his business might be over before it really began.

on a huge variety of roles and different tasks in order to make ends meet. However, as the business develops and profits increase, the owner has far more to lose by risk-taking, and risk-taking strategies tend to become more cautious. David Gold, the multimillionaire, for instance, owns several racehorses. As mentioned earlier, he doesn't bet on them, purely because he calculates that his chances of success are low. However, he also jointly owns a football club, Birmingham City, which some might say is a truly risky venture. Nevertheless, he knows a great deal about football, but also in any football game the odds of

learn from the millionaires

Chris Gorman was doing exceedingly well as a mobile phone salesman, taking his Scottish division from the lowest performing region to the highest in under a year. So when he announced that he was quitting his job, leaving security and salary and borrowing £25,000 to go into partnership with Richard Emanuel, of DX Communications, a one-stop mobile phone store, his friends thought he was mad. 'It was a huge risk,' he admits. 'But it was something I felt I had to do. And having been successful I had the self-belief to know I could be again.'

However, things did not go smoothly. The business needed more money, so Chris borrowed again, guaranteeing his house against the loan. He intended to tell his wife, 'but she was pregnant, so it didn't seem to be the right time.' Somehow it didn't ever seem to be the right time to tell her, until things took a dive and they were only several days from possible liquidation. Chris came home on a Friday night, desolate and unable to sleep. He still hadn't told Mary, and the business and the house were on the line. He began to think about where they would stay once their house was repossessed – with her parents, perhaps, or back in a council house or ... 'Then I realised there was no point in me thinking about where I'd be staying because when Mary did find out, I'd be out!'

Fortunately, another bank stepped in and Chris eventually told his wife about the guarantee – after he'd made his first million! So would he undertake such a risk again? He says no. Now he has more to lose, so the risks need to be less. Nevertheless, he is adamant that risk-taking is vital in a new enterprise and that even when growing a business, you have to be prepared to take the risks to get the rewards.

winning, drawing or losing are much lower odds than for horse racing, where numerous horses can result in a plethora of different outcomes.

Indeed, the degree of risk-taking varies hugely between business people. However, all believe it is a necessity to take calculated risks to reap rewards. For some, risk-taking is a buzz, for others a necessity. But none will shrink from risks they believe they have calculated well and which they believe will pay off, simply on the basis that risk is involved.

spreading the risk – having a partner

Most of the business people featured in this book did not start up entirely by themselves. David Quayle, the Q of B&Q, linked up with Richard Block, the B in B&Q. Karan Bilimoria and Sahar Hashemi both had partners. Chris Gorman joined Richard Emanuel to jointly create a hugely successful company, DX Communications.

Many businesses start as partnerships, though few remain that way. Often where partnerships remain it is because each individual brings different skills, but an equal commitment. Priscilla and Antonio Carluccio, the founder of Carluccio's delicatessens and caffés, are married, but both have clearly defined – and different – roles within the business. Tom Hartley Junior bought his way into his father's business, which has left Tom Senior with more time to pursue his other business, Park Homes, while still being part of the car business. Sunseeker International is a family concern with both Robert Braithwaite's brother and daughter in the business.

persistence

Persistence is a key attribute of all successful people. You can't succeed in sport, entertainment or corporate life if you give up the first time you lose a game, are not selected at audition or get made redundant. However, entrepreneurs are perhaps the most persistent of all. This is because they keep going when most people would willingly give up.

exercise: thinking about risk

It helps to know your risk threshold before you start a business. Before you decide how much you are willing to risk, ask yourself these questions:

1 What am I willing to risk on this venture? What am I not willing to risk?

2 Am I willing to risk my savings on this or another venture? Am I willing to risk my house? Or be seriously in debt? Which of these three is the least unappealing option for me? How can this help me to decide my financing priorities (savings, bank loan, business angel, etc)?

3 How much time am I willing to risk on this venture? Am I willing to work for a couple of years for what may be effectively nothing? Are the potential rewards too good to miss?

4 What is the worst that can happen? Is it worth the risk?

5 What is the best possible outcome? Is it worth the risk?

Knowing your tolerance of risk will help you decide your future direction. If you are risk-averse, for instance, but feel you have the other qualities required to run a business, you may be interested in franchising where you effectively buy into an established brand and build up your own name within that franchise.

They keep going despite the odds. Looked at from the outside their persistence, while admirable, can even seem irrational. Not only do they keep banging their heads against brick walls, they actually headbutt their way through the wall to the success which lies on the other side.

Why are they able to be so persistent? Partly it is because they are sustained by their self-belief. The task may seem huge to others, but they know they can do it. They are also sustained by belief in their product

Entrepreneurs rarely take no for an answer

or their vision of success. This persistence is vital in the early years when things are roughest, or when there is a downturn in the market, or finance is difficult. Not one of the millionaires in this book has had a uniformly easy ride. All of them spoke of knock-backs, near-misses, disappointments, times when it was a continual struggle.

Persistence is vitally important when it comes to obtaining finance. One study revealed that it is access to finance that can make or break a new business. However, persistence is often the key to finding finance. If you plan to finance your business yourself, you will need to save persistently to do it. If you wish to find bank, business angel or venture capital funding, you may need considerable persistence to persuade anyone to back you. For instance, Sahar Hashemi of Coffee Republic was turned down by 22 banks before being accepted.

Persistence is vital when it comes to finding finance

Indeed, according to the Tulip research two-thirds of entrepreneurs say they rarely take no for an answer. This is considerably higher than for professionals, company directors and those working in the public service. When it comes to setting up a business, persistence really pays.

problem-solving

One in ten new businesses go bust, in certain sectors more (one in three within the first three years of the restaurant business, for example). In order to start a new business and keep it running through those first dangerous years, an entrepreneur will need to overcome a whole host

learn from the millionaires

One of the highlights of Robert Braithwaite's career was watching the James Bond film, *The World Is Not Enough*. It was not the gorgeous Lycra-clad baddy Bond babe leading a speedboat chase that entranced him, but one of the boats, a Hawk 34, one of Braithwaite's own Sunseeker models. 'After they'd seen that film even children in China now know what a Sunseeker is,' says Braithwaite, a rugged man, happiest in his boatyard.

International recognition and a glamorous product (Roger Moore also appropriately has a Sunseeker) are a far and happy cry from the days when Braithwaite started out, with a passion for boating, a £5,000 loan from his father's business partner, a team of seven – and no orders.

The first few years, he admits, were hellish. He was working seven days a week, but orders were few and he felt he was getting nowhere. He remembers a boat show in Stockholm where he didn't speak a word of the language and was just desperate to sell the boats from the stand and go home. 'I did think of giving up,' he admits. 'But it was my vision that just kept me going.'

The turning point came when he exhibited at the London Boat Show, with a range of boats. A visitor to the stand, the former Formula One racing driver Henry Taylor, liked one. He said that if it could be made in a different colour and with an added sun-bed, he would buy it. Adding the glamour element helped sales and, from that, Robert learnt a valuable lesson – 'Never build one model, build three. People want a choice.' He began to expand his range and the business started to take off.

of obstacles, many of which they have never come across before. For instance, they will need to find finance, source suppliers, find staff, understand employment contracts and, most of all, persuade customers to buy.

If you think of starting a new business as somewhat akin to a hurdles race, many will fall at the first hurdle such as finding finance, a few more will fall at the production stage and yet others will be somersaulted over by other issues. This leaves only a few who will complete the course.

In order to make it to the finishing line, you need to be good not only at identifying problems, but finding creative solutions. However, fortunately, most entrepreneurs are great problem-solvers, able to think over, around, underneath and straight through the middle of obstacles that would floor others.

There are two main reasons for this. The first is that most of us see the world in a certain structured way with rules, overt and covert, that we adhere to almost subconsciously. According to Dr Atkinson, the entrepreneur's world view is much less hindered by these unspoken rules. He gives the example of an airline check-in queue. When people arrive at an airport, they automatically join the check-in queue although there are no signs saying that they have to queue to check in. Theoretically, one could just push to the front ahead of everyone else. But most of us don't. Even if it may mean missing our flights. Entrepreneurs, on the other hand, would have no qualms about telling people that they need to go first – and doing so.

Entrepreneurs think 'outside the box'

Entrepreneurs are essentially rule-breakers

In our society, anyone who is prepared to think around those unwritten rules or unspoken conventions for the way things are done, will be able to find more efficient ways to operate – short cuts that can really make all the difference. Entrepreneurs are adept at identifying – and taking – these short cuts and bending rules to their limit. The fact

learn from the millionaires

Mandy Haberman believes that the best ideas come from everyday life. Indeed, she had the idea for the Anywayup Cup in a friend's living room. She was visiting a friend with a pristine new cream carpet – and a visiting toddler. Watching the mother repeatedly dive frantically and unsuccessfully, like a character in a farce, to prevent the toddler's cup of Ribena creating a snail trail on the brand new carpet made Mandy think there must be a better way. She decided to try to come up with a product she knew mothers would love – a beaker designed for toddlers that wouldn't spill even if it was held upside down.

The idea was simple, but the mechanics are extremely difficult, and it took Mandy five whole years of designing, redesigning and perfecting, from coming up with the idea to getting it on to the market. 'I knew I could do it, and I knew it wouldn't be quick. But I also knew that if I carried on it would work.'

that a rule exists does not mean they feel the need to obey it.

This gives them greater power to think 'outside the box' and to find new and more efficient ways of doing things and of

Millionaires dislike rules and regulations, written or otherwise – they do not respect convention for convention's sake

getting around problems. If you see a rule as something that is working to your disadvantage, but that can be evaded or avoided, you are in a much better position to circumvent it, than someone who is essentially scared off by the rule from tackling that obstacle. For instance, Mandy Haberman was told by one divisional head of a supermarket that they would not buy her Anywayup Cup. Rather than accept this, she sent the cup, full of juice, directly to the buyer. The buyer saw the cup – and more importantly that the juice hadn't spilt – and bought it. This willingness to try a second way of doing things if the first fails is typical of entrepreneurs.

The other reason that entrepreneurs are able to problem-solve so successfully is their essentially optimistic nature. They believe that there has to be a solution and they look for it until they find it. Many are lateral thinkers – that may be one reason why, despite often being very bright, they have not done so well at school. Others are so driven that they are just determined to mow down any obstacle, even if it's iceberg-sized. Interestingly, on the problem-solving day for the *Mind of a Millionaire* series, the control group of millionaire entrepreneurs scored significantly higher on problem-solving aptitude than the normal citizens. But perhaps the award for the most enterprising of all entrepreneurs should go to David Gold. He was desperate to learn the piano, but somehow could never ever master it. So he bought a pianola – a mechanised piano that plays itself. Now he tinkles happily on the ivories, enjoying the music and fooling guests that he's playing. Even his mum was taken in!

Below are a variety of problem-solving questions designed by Dr Adrian Atkinson scientifically designed to test your problem-solving abilities and stretch them. Have a go and see how you do:

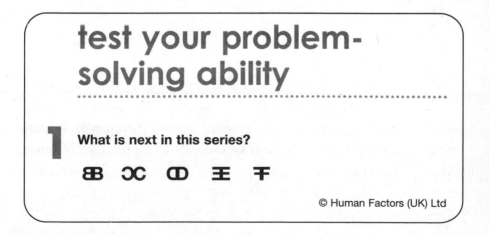

test your problem-solving ability

1 **What is next in this series?**

ᗺB ƆC ᗡD Ŧ Ŧ

© Human Factors (UK) Ltd

2 **Using one straight line only, make this number equal to 32**

1 2 8 4

3 **Complete the phrase or saying:**

9 P in the SS   3 B M

2 Q in a H   26 L in the A

14 L in a S   366 D in a LY

7 W of the AW   52 C in a P

10,000 M of the G O D of Y   1 Q of E

32 P on a C B   1 W on a U

11 P in a F T   5 O of the W

360 D in a C   57 H V

4 **What letter should replace the question mark to complete the word?**

E T E R N U
N R P E E ?

5 **What is half of 8? Find three ways to answer this question.**

(*Solutions on page 122*)

business challenges

There are no wrong or right answers to these questions:

1 Develop a new type of saucepan that will be safer in the home e.g. not easily knocked over, etc.

What business could you start tomorrow with no money?

 Invent a way of automating ironing of clothes for the domestic user.

 How could you convey the smell of a perfume to a television audience?

 Think of three strange, unusual uses for a polystyrene cup. How would you market the product in this new application?

life challenges

 If you broke all contact with family and friends how would you set up a new life in another country?

 How could you make yourself more attractive?

 What are the five things you have achieved in your life so far?

 What are the five things you still want to achieve in life?

 What are the three biggest errors or failures you have had in the past 10 years? What beneficial consequences came out of these?

(Marking on page 124)

the solutions that made all the difference

karan bilimoria and the mystery of the beer the buyers couldn't try

If you were a restaurant owner and an unknown person walked off the street trying to persuade you to buy a new beer on the basis of its unique taste and less gassy quality, you'd try a sip, or ten, before you could be persuaded. Right?

Except that as Karan Bilimoria found, inviting restaurant owners to taste the product often wasn't possible when it came to supplying Indian restaurants. Two-thirds of the owners of Indian restaurants cannot drink alcohol as it is forbidden by their religion. That meant he was trying to persuade them to take an unknown brand, from an unknown seller, with a taste that would also remain unknown to them.

The solution?

Karan left a couple of sample bottles for the restaurant owner to give to regular customers for them to try. The experiment was an outstanding success with a 100% reordering rate.

Another major obstacle was that Indian breweries only brewed beer in big bottles, unlike British beer. 'It was an obstacle, but I turned it into a selling point,' says Karan.

He told the restaurateurs that this was the true way that beer was sold in India, so it would be more authentic. What's more the bigger bottles would encourage people both to drink more and to help themselves, leaving the waiters to get on with serving other customers. The restaurateurs accepted his logic and today, over two-thirds of Cobra Beer is sold in large bottles.

david quayle – cash flow quirks at B&Q

Cash flow can be a major problem for start-up businesses, as you may well have to pay for goods before you've sold them. David Quayle opened B&Q with a limited stock, but he found a smart way to ease cash flow problems. He discovered that if he ordered stock the last week of December, it would be delivered the first week of January, but he wouldn't have to pay for it until the last week of February – by which time he'd sold it! This is a canny way to deal with the cash flow problems that can beset a start-up business.

robert braithwaite – seeking more of the sun

Some years back, Robert Braithwaite found that recession meant orders for Sunseeker craft were tailing off, despite innovations and improved designs.

His solution was to move into building the biggest boats of all, the super-cruiser market for floating mansions that can cost nearly £5 million each. This may seem paradoxical, as you may think bigger boats would be harder to sell than smaller ones in a difficult market. However, Robert noticed that there was less competition in these areas and more room for building an innovative brand. As 99% of his boats are exported, there was also potential for new markets. This bold solution paid off and Sunseeker continued to grow.

sarah tremellen – going for bust

When Sarah, a vivacious woman, first set up Bravissimo, there was a rival company only a few miles away. The rival had been going for some time and, angered by another player on the scene, persuaded the bra suppliers that they should not deal with another company.

The solution?

Sarah and her original partner (who has since left the business) realised that it was vital to keep in touch with the bra companies. Rather than asking them to supply her outright, she asked her prospective suppliers to give her advice about bras and keep her abreast of new developments. The idea was to stay in touch and gradually persuade them that she was a serious contender. Meanwhile, she worked on turning Bravissimo from a company selling bras into a lifestyle concept, thus differentiating it from their rivals. Early editions of the catalogue had articles featuring celebrities with big breasts, with fashion and lifestyle advice. 'We tried to make it more of a celebration of having big breasts, a brand, not just about selling bras,' says Sarah.

Sarah's tenacity and her original way of approaching the market impressed the suppliers, and they agreed to supply Bravissimo – provided that they were based in a different area.

Sarah solved this problem by using her parents' home in Oxford as her company base. She had the bras and orders delivered there and three times a week she or her partner would drive the sixty miles to pick up orders, send out bras and check the mail. She even had her phone number rerouted via Oxford. 'It was a turning point in my life,' says Sarah. 'I'd always been a quitter, but I became tenacious because I was determined to make this work.'

After four months, Bravissimo was selling so many bras that the suppliers agreed to let them operate from wherever they liked.

alexander amosu – ringing the changes

Alexander Amosu had been selling his ringtones to an ever-growing circle of friends and acquaintances but he knew that to make a commercial success of it, he needed to have technical backing to be able to produce for a larger market. The problem was that he didn't have any money to pay them. He approached telecoms companies and his enthusiasm, plus the product, was so persuasive that one agreed to make the application for free. Alexander later discovered that they sold similar applications to rivals, but he feels that if he hadn't been able to get the applications made, he might not have been able to finance them and the business may not have got off the ground at all!

chris gorman – scotching problems

When Chris Gorman arrived in Scotland as a mobile phone salesman, he knew it would be a challenge. But there was one problem he didn't anticipate. On his first day, he attempted to make a sale. The customer seemed extremely interested, then said that although Chris was pushing all the right buttons, he just couldn't bring himself to buy from an Englishman!

Chris knew he needed to find a way to increase sales. His solution was to spend several evenings each week in the library, working out who the best prospects were and how each of those companies would benefit from buying from him.

This tailor-made approach was, not surprisingly, highly successful and Scotland went from the worst-performing sales region to the best in less than a year. By having a finely tuned sales strategy and company knowledge Chris was able to overcome any residual prejudice about his ancestry.

facing up to failure

Risk-taking brings big rewards, but it can also lead to big failures. One of the most interesting characteristics of entrepreneurs is their resilience. They do fail – but they are able to brush off that failure and get on to the next thing, with an insouciance most of us envy. For most of them failure is often not a failure. Indeed, several interviewed said that they only regarded something as failure if they made the same mistake twice.

'I don't perceive things that don't work as failure. Failure is when you have no options. Even someone in a prison cell has options. Don't give in, just find a new route.' RICHARD PROUT

An entrepreneurial type is unlikely to be put off doing anything he believes will work, by a background risk of failure. And while many non-entrepreneurs do not apply for jobs they covet or try

running a sideline

It may be that having read this chapter, you feel that you are not willing to take on the commitment of having your own business. You may also decide that you do not wish to climb the corporate ladder all the way to the top. However, you may still want to increase income. While becoming seriously rich without any effort only happens if you win the lottery or kiss a frog in a fairytale (unless you are an heir or prepared to marry one), there are ways to use your skills to increase your income by a steady margin. Here are some ideas to get you thinking.

- How many hours a week do you spend on leisure time, chores, sleep? How many of these hours could be turned to profit without becoming utterly wretched?

- What are the skills you possess that could earn money? These may be skills that you use in your day job, such as IT skills, or hobbies in your spare time, such as gardening. For instance, if you work on an IT helpdesk, you could offer IT training or help to small businesses locally. If you are a keen gardener, you could try and sell speciality plants or herbs into a local greengrocer or from home. Go through each of your skills carefully until you come up with one that seems the most lucrative and is exciting enough to motivate yourself to do it.

- Research the field you want to enter before you start. Assess demand locally, the rate for the job, competition, etc. Do as much research as you can so you can target yourself effectively. Then set goals for your small-scale enterprise.

- Be persistent – finding the first customer is the hardest. Note the skills that entrepreneurs need to have and use them. The fact that your goal is smaller doesn't mean the same principles don't hold true.

- Gradually increase the scope of your goals and your income as you succeed.

something difficult because they might fail, this would be anathema to entrepreneurs.

Entrepreneurs see failure either as a necessary step on the road to success, or they do not see it as failure at all, simply as something that 'didn't work out', 'wasn't quite right' or as a 'learning experience'. Most expect to have a few failures. Richard Prout, for instance, points to the example of a salesman friend of his who awards himself £10 every time he makes a call, whether the call results in a sale or not. That's because the more failures he has, the more successes he also has.

Risk-taking is vital – but there is always the chance of failure

Indeed, in many respects entrepreneurs are like sportsmen. Their whole life is about the pursuit of winning, but they know that that has to mean that occasionally they must lose. Just like sportsmen, the entrepreneur who wins every single game has not yet been discovered. However, academic research suggests that one characteristic which divides successful entrepreneurs from the unsuccessful is that the successful ones know when to quit. If something isn't working out, they will abandon it, persisting only with those they know have potential. Indeed, many of the entrepreneurs featured in this book have had business failures. David Quayle, for instance, admits that he never gets into any business without working out how he would get out if it doesn't work. (He feels he learnt from buying a bone china factory, which didn't pay off.) Chris Gorman admits to several failures including a recording studio that cost him three-quarters of a million pounds of his own money.

'Without the risk there wouldn't be the thrill. If there was no risk there would be no pleasure.'
TOM HARTLEY SENIOR

However, there are some entrepreneurs who are motivated by a fear of failure. Unlike those who are equable about failure, this group dread the sort of spectacular failure that might deprive them of their wealth. Their solution is either to diversify into several businesses, thus spreading their risk, or if they are a one-strand business, simply to work and problem-solve their way out of any major hitches. 'Failure is not an option' might well be their motto.

the magic moment

For many of the entrepreneurs profiled here, months – and sometimes years – of hard work preceded their success. Here are some of their recollections of the time when they knew they had made it:

David Quayle vividly remembers the moment he knew he was on to a winner. In March 1969, he opened the first B&Q. Just before Easter, traditionally the best time for DIY devotees, he took advertising in the local newspapers. 'On Easter Saturday they were literally queuing halfway round the shop. At my previous company we thought we'd done well if we took £300 on a Saturday. That Easter we were taking £1,000 a day.'

As this was before the days of electronic tills, they had to devise a system to speed throughput. David and his partner would call out the items, the woman on the till would key them in and pass the receipt on to another woman who had the cash drawer and would dole out change. 'It was hugely exciting,' David recalls. He also feels a certain pride recalling that in 2003, B&Q stores took over £105 million on the same day!

'A deal is a deal. Even if someone comes and offers me more money in the afternoon, the original deal sticks. I am what you see.'
TOM HARTLEY SENIOR

For **Priscilla Carluccio**, the day she knew Carluccio's caffé would work as a concept was the day she opened their very first branch near head office.

For months Antonio and Priscilla had struggled to find finance, and despite their experience, both in catering and business, had been told by outsiders that the concept might not work. However, Priscilla recalls that from the very first day the caffé opened it was overflowing. 'I'd go in and talk to people and there was a wonderful mix. One of the customers used it three times a day to have meetings, one spread his papers and worked there, there was a woman breastfeeding. It was just what we envisaged, a place with no rules, where you can eat breakfast in the evening if you want, and welcoming all sorts of people.'

For **Chris Gorman**, a defining moment was when he made his first million only a few days before his 30th birthday. 'I'd been telling people I'd be a millionaire before I was 30 from when I was 21,' he says. 'So when I actually saw the cheque it was a great feeling.'

Basil Newby says the first time he realised he was wealthy was when he went into the bank 'and they gave me a gold credit card, with no limit on it.'

why they succeeded

entrepreneurs' beliefs about the qualities that made them successful

1   Hard work (90%)
2   Being honest and trustworthy (85%)
3   Enjoyment of work (82%)
4   Getting along with people (82%)
5   Taking opportunities (81%)
6   Being my own boss (72%)
7   Intelligence (69%)
8   Being well disciplined and dedicated to success (68%)
9   Being physically fit and well/employing good people (67%)
10   Having a supportive partner (66%)

which type of entrepreneur are you?

Of the entrepreneurs who start and run their own businesses, there are several different types.

serial entrepreneurs

These entrepreneurs will start and run several businesses, in several different fields, and will often have more than one on the go at any one time. They love the fact that they are in control of their lives and it is very important to them to be able to buy whatever they choose, whether that is a motor cruiser, Rolls-Royce or villa. For them, the point is that they could, if they wanted to. The archetype of this kind of entrepreneur is, of course, Richard Branson whose empires encompass everything from music to transport. Chris Gorman, whose ventures have ranged from mobile phones to The Gadget Shop, is another serial entrepreneur, as is David Gold. David freely admits it is the fear of poverty and the need to be sure that he will never suffer it again that drives him.

theme entrepreneurs

These are eager to be the best in a certain field which they know a great deal about. That might mean building an international brand, using their academic knowledge to fuel their business success, or following a particular passion. They want to be celebrated in their specialist field, and to produce the best in it. Antonio Carluccio, the chef now running his own brand of successful restaurants with his wife Priscilla, is a good example of this type of entrepreneur, as is Robert Braithwaite of Sunseeker International, who says that he wants Sunseeker to become a brand. 'I want people to think Sunseeker when they say boat.'

social entrepreneurs

This type wants to create a business so they can run it in ways that they believe accord with their social responsibility. Often their approach is distinguished by a different management style to contemporary models with strong emphasis on both the team and the way in which they are managed. Anita Roddick, founder of The Body Shop, is an excellent example. She used her brand and stores to help promote the ethical causes she believed in. Julian Richer of Richer Sounds, who has won several awards for his working practices, has holiday homes specifically for the use of employees and even lends his Rolls-Royce to a different shop worker each week.

revenge entrepreneurs

These men and women are driven by an urge to prove themselves, to overcome obstacles that they perceive have been put in their way. They may have been dyslexic at school, or under-performed or not been given opportunities. Some immigrant entrepreneurs fall into this category. Their parents did not get the opportunities and breaks they should have done, despite their drive and intelligence, but their children are determined not only to obtain the opportunities their parents never had, but to exploit their full potential.

'intrapreneurs'

This kind share many of the same characteristics as entrepreneurs – but they are more averse to risk. They wouldn't dream, for instance, of offering their home as security for starting a business, or pledging all their savings. They are best working for corporations where talent, innovation, new ideas and some risk-taking are welcomed, but the personal risks are lower.

which type of entrepreneur are you?

This questionnaire, created by Dr Adrian Atkinson, is designed to tell you what kind of entrepreneur you are likely to be. It is in two parts with three questions in each part.

Read the scenario for question 1 and imagine you are in the situation described. Then read both of the descriptions of the a and b opportunities and choose which of the a or b opportunity associated with scenario 1 you think is best for you.

Make a decision for question 2 and then for question 3.

part a

1 You work in a manufacturing company which has three factories in Europe and three in China. You have assisted the Production Director in developing and implementing the strategy for moving some of the manufacturing to China. You personally see an opportunity to provide other manufacturing companies with a consultancy service for deciding on the strategy for moving manufacturing to China or other lower-cost areas of the world.

Do you ...

a) Spend your weekends putting together a business plan for the creation of a subsidiary consultancy business to present to the CEO in three months' time? This would be a new type of business for the company but you would be able to show that it would produce far greater profit margin than the existing business.

b) Extend the mortgage on your house to finance yourself and hand in your notice to start your own consultancy business? This business will provide advice and help to companies wanting to set up in countries where there is a significant lower cost of employment. Clients to your consultancy would be seeking manufacturing facilities or the provision of services such as computer programming.

2 You work for a large international company as Human Resources Manager. Four months ago you were assigned to a team to review the role of HR and decide how much of the HR function should be outsourced. Your review team will be recommending that the company outsource much of the HR function to a provider who can supply multiple functions including payroll and staff selection. This will change the nature of the company's core HR team and reduce the number of HR personnel by half.

Do you ...
a) Work hard to set yourself up as indispensable to your company and thereby ensure that you not only retain your job but try to soon become head of the core HR team?
b) One of the providers of HR outsourcing offers you a senior job with them to help develop the company in what appears to be a competitive but growing market. Do you accept their job offer even though you would no longer be an HR professional but there is an opportunity to learn new skills in sales and marketing?

3 You are 35 years old and have been Managing Director of a £10 million turnover company for three years. It is a subsidiary of a group which the new CEO has reorganised so that your job has become redundant. There has not been enough challenge in this job especially in the area of international business development which is what you enjoy. You have been given three months' notice. You have a spouse and two young children and a mortgage.

Do you ...

a) Immediately place your name with search companies and look for a job as the Managing Director of a £20 million or more turnover company? Your next company would need to have the opportunity for you to expand its sales into Europe or the USA so that you can apply your international business development ability though you are yet to prove yourself in this area.

b) Five years ago you had a good idea for a business, so you take the opportunity to start this business. You have a friend who is retired and is willing to provide enough money to finance the first 18 months of the business and will be the Finance Director of the new company. You also have a little money to put into the business.

If you score 2 or 3 a's then you are likely to be an intrapreneur (see page 115).

If you score 2 or 3 b's then go to part b.

part b

1 You have two degrees in biochemistry. The biochemistry business you started six years ago is now very profitable and you have a turnover of £20 million and 200 employees. You are still needed as chairman and CEO but you have a very good managing director. Recently you have come across two other business opportunities. You could personally provide the funding for one of them.

Which would you choose?

a) This business would provide a highly specialised service to pharmaceutical companies. The expertise your new company would provide is not normally found within pharmaceutical companies. You would need to bring at least 20 highly specialised biochemists together from around the world and provide expensive high-tech equipment. You believe it would become highly profitable after four years.

b) You were impressed by the young psychologist who approached you to be involved in the setting up of an internet business. It would provide recruitment, selection and employee surveys to major companies. The business plan says that it would take 18 months to develop the IT platform and test it. Then it would require a team of 10 psychologists to market, sell and deliver the services. The young psychologist expects the business to begin delivering to clients after two years and to be highly profitable soon after.

2 You have a Masters degree in Brewing and Wine and are recognised as an entrepreneur because of the way you have built your business. You started nine years ago at the age of 27, with one shop selling food and wines from around the world. These shops now sell packages for themed dinner parties such as a Mexican evening, and you now have 18 shops around Europe with a turnover of £11 million and good profitability. You have recently sold this business and now have a large amount of spare money to fund a new business. You have identified two opportunities, only one of which you can fund.

Which do you choose?

a) An excellent, quality beer producer in Hungary requires investment if it is to significantly increase its output. The company would agree for you to purchase it and become the chairman and chief executive. The company has a turnover of £2 million and has 60 employees. It is not known outside Hungary but is recognised for its high-quality beer within Hungary.

b) A small specialist travel company has approached you to invest in them in order to expand. They would also want you to be the chairman and managing director. They specialise in taking groups to unusual places in the world for people to experience something very different. The company believes it could become an internet-based club for people around the world interested in unusual events and places. For example, there are many volcanoes in the world and they take groups to visit five volcanoes in two weeks. Their turnover at present is £4.5 million with 30 employees but they also have to pay the local assistants and the experts who accompany the groups.

3 When you left school you joined a company which gave you training to become a computer programmer. You very quickly became a specialist in security systems to stop hackers getting into databases. You set up your own computer security company when you were 28 and developed systems for network as well as database security. You specialised in aerospace and the defence industries and built the company up to 300 people and £40 million turnover. You have recently sold the business and are looking to get involved in another business.

Which do you choose?

a) A company in the USA has developed a physical screening mesh which is moulded into the inside of computer monitors and the metal case which surrounds the computer. This stops the radiation from the computer and therefore prevents anyone being able to pick up what is going on in the computer. The turnover is about £30 million every year with profits around £5 million. They need investment in manufacturing equipment to be able to produce far higher volumes at much lower cost. They also need to carry out research to develop the next generation of their product especially for the mobile phone market.

b) You have been approached by a small group of ten treasure hunters who identify and then dive on wrecks to recover the contents of the ships. They have had some limited success with income of £1 million last year and a profit of £50,000. However, at present they only have normal scuba diving equipment which limits them to wrecks no more than 40 metres deep. They now have asked if you would invest and become the chairman and managing director to purchase the high-tech equipment required to dive safely to much greater depths. This would allow them to travel to sites anywhere in the world with the possibility of recovering millions of pounds' worth of gold, silver and porcelain from just one wreck. They would also have to employ some specialist divers on a contract basis and hire appropriate large dive ships. However, they could make profits every year of anywhere between £5 million and £50 million.

If you scored two or three a's then you are likely to be a theme entrepreneur (see page 114).

If you scored two or three b's then you are likely to be a serial entrepreneur (see page 114).

Solutions to quiz (page 82)

1. If you chose **c** you are someone who sees opportunities and thinks about how to use them.

2. If you chose **c** you are someone on the lookout for opportunities as you believe you can influence events.

3. If you chose **a** you are aware of the value of creating opportunities.

4. If you answered **a** you are someone who is willing to act and grab any opportunity.

5. If you picked **c** you are someone who is eager to start their own business and are just looking for the right opportunity.

Solutions to quiz (page 103)

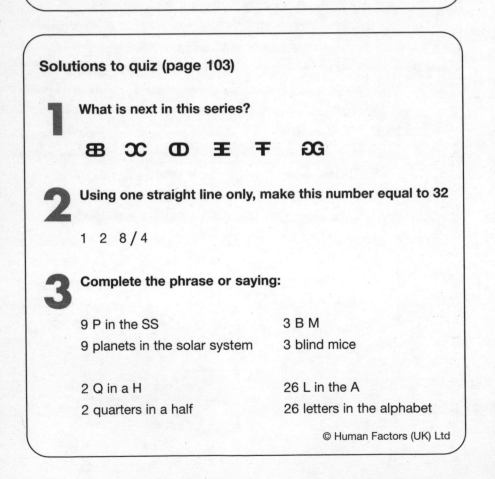

1 **What is next in this series?**

8B 3C CD 3E 7F 9G

2 **Using one straight line only, make this number equal to 32**

1 2 8 / 4

3 **Complete the phrase or saying:**

9 P in the SS
9 planets in the solar system

3 B M
3 blind mice

2 Q in a H
2 quarters in a half

26 L in the A
26 letters in the alphabet

14 L in a S
14 lines in a sonnet

366 D in a LY
366 days in a leap year

7 W of the AW
7 wonders of the ancient world

52 C in a P
52 cards in a pack

10,000 M of the G O D of Y
10,000 Men of the Grand
Old Duke of York

1 Q of E
1 Queen of England

32 P on a C B
32 pieces on a chess board

1 W on a U
1 wheel on a unicycle

11 P in a F T
11 players in a football team

5 O of the W
5 oceans of the world

360 D in a C
360 degrees in a circle

57 H V
57 Heinz varieties

 What letter should replace the question mark to complete the word?

E T E R N U
N R P E E n

 What is half of 8? Find three ways to answer this question.

4
3 (if cut in half vertically)
0 (if cut in half horizontally)

marking: business challenges and life challenges (pages 104–105)

Entrepreneurs will persevere with creative problem solving until they answer all of these questions correctly.

Entrepreneurs will enjoy trying to answer the questions in business challenges and life challenges. Non-entrepreneurs will not persevere with the business challenges and tend to avoid the life challenges questions. There are no uniquely correct answers to the last two sections.

© Human Factors (UK) Ltd

ms millionaire

and why there are so few of them

*'Women are like tea bags, put them in
hot water and they get stronger.'*

ELEANOR ROOSEVELT

When it comes to wealth, it's still a man's world out there. While
nearly 70% of women are in paid work, only 7% of Britain's richest are
women – and that includes those who've married or inherited wealth.
If you imagine wealth as a world map, men are China and Russia and
women are a tiny dot in the Indian Ocean.

Tulip Financial Research estimates that there are 30,000 female
millionaires in the UK, out of 150,000 in total.

At first, this might seem odd given that women are striding
through the ranks of management. However, women are more likely
to make their money through management, rather than running their
own business – and business people tend to be richer than corporate
players. What's more, when it comes to the very highest ranks of

management, women are seriously behind. In FTSE 100 companies only one in 40 executive posts are held by women and only 7% of directorships are held by women. Nearly 40% of top companies have no woman on the board.

Just one in five millionaires are female

In business, the story is even more pronounced. Only 13% of the millionaire entrepreneurs were female. This is especially surprising when you consider that women start a third of all small businesses. However, despite the well-publicised success stories such as Dame Stephanie Shirley, Anita Roddick and Linda Bennett (the well-heeled owner of LK Bennett, the fashion and shoe shop), it seems that for the majority of women, when it comes to business, small is beautiful. Indeed, female entrepreneurs tend to be less wealthy than their male counterparts.

'Turning an idea into reality is the most satisfying feeling there is.'
MANDY HABERMAN

So why is this? One of the reasons may be that women simply don't want to make the sacrifices that men are prepared to make. As women still bear the greater responsibility for their children and, indeed, often for their partner's welfare, it is likely that they are simply opting out of the twenty-four/seven commitment that the most senior jobs demand.

Women are more likely to make money through management than starting their own business

However, it's encouraging to note that 77% of female millionaires are co-habiting or married – so clearly it is possible, if difficult, to sustain a high-flying career and stable partnership.

Female entrepreneurs also tend to differ from their male counterparts. They often have better people skills and are more people-focused. For that reason, they often prefer to run manageable-sized businesses, rather than mega-conglomerates, where they still feel they know the key staff and retain a personal involvement in the business. They are often theme entrepreneurs too, preferring to work long-term with a product they really believe in, rather than moving from business to business as a butterfly dips from flower to flower.

However, the fact that women tend not to grow multinational businesses or brands may also be because of the degree of risk involved. The Tulip survey shows that female business owners are considerably more cautious than their male counterparts and more risk-averse – which means they are also less likely to gain the greatest financial rewards. Put bluntly, fewer women have the necessary millionaire mindset and values.

Women millionaires are generally poorer than their male counter-parts. Mr Millionaire is, on average, 53% more wealthy than his female counterpart, and his income is nearly 20% higher. (Female millionaires are worth an average of £1.7 million, as opposed to the male average of £2.6 million. The 'average' male millionaire has an income of £112,000 annually, as compared to an 'average' millionaire female income of £95,000.)

Women entrepreneurs are more risk-averse

While a disparity in income can be explained in terms of more men reaching director level, or becoming serial entrepreneurs, which is often where the really serious money lies, it is harder to explain the difference in assets.

a different attitude

One of the reasons why wealthy women may be less wealthy than men is actually that they have a different attitude. While their number one priority is, like men, to have money for savings and investments, they do seem to be less motivated by money as a concept, a benchmark of success and a way of scoring their own worth. For instance, when women millionaires were asked about their youthful ambitions, the most popular ambition was to be part of a happy family, with a third of the women saying this had been their number one target – as

learn from the millionaires

Mandy Haberman always thought of herself as unassertive, someone who shrank from conflict the way others avoid ill-fitting shoes. But when an international company infringed her patent, she found a resolve she never realised she had. 'I'd struggled and struggled and built up this business and if I hadn't enforced my patent other companies would have infringed it, too.'

She held a family conference and, backed by her husband and children, decided to take the company to court. She knew that the stakes were high. Not only was her business on the line, but, if she lost, her children would have to leave their private schools and the whole family would be affected. For some male entrepreneurs, this sort of risk is par for the course, but Mandy admits that it gave her plenty of sleepless nights.

The court case for patent infringement was heard in December – which meant a nail-biting wait until after Christmas to get the results – a full and complete victory. 'It did change me,' she says. 'I've learnt that I'm a fighter and it's given me a great deal of confidence.'

Like many female entrepreneurs, Mandy did not consciously start out with the intention of building a major business. Indeed, her first entrepreneurial venture was founded out of necessity. Her child, Emily, was born with feeding difficulties and Mandy was told she would not be allowed out of hospital until there was an effective way to feed her. Mandy, a designer by profession, invented a feeding device – the Haberman Feeder – which fed her own child effectively. She realised it had wider implications, although it took her five years to get the concept from invention to the market place. Even then, she says that, 'In the early days, in some of the hospitals, there was terrible resistance to change. The attitude was we feed our babies this way because we've always done it this way, and I'd go along and say, it doesn't have to be like that.'

For Mandy being her own boss is very important. Indeed, one of the driving forces that led her to become an inventor-entrepreneur was her wish to earn as much as her husband and yet still achieve the sort of control over her own life that being self-employed entails. However, she admits that it took her a while to get used to being wealthy. 'If I want a dress, I go out and buy it, but it took me a long time to learn to do that. When you haven't had a lot of money for a large part of your life, there is an awful lot of adjustment. Of course, the money is good, but it's the icing, not the cake.'

She also feels she has been fortunate in having the support of her husband, an academic, right from the start. However, she also has made a conscious effort to work from home in order to ease the problems of balancing work and family commitments. 'I think for a lot of men work is about climbing the ladder and earning lots of money, and I don't think women are as concerned about that. I saw a problem and I wanted to solve it.'

opposed to only 15% of men. By contrast, however, while over a quarter of men said their ambition was to be financially secure, less than 20% of women had this ambition.

Women millionaires rated family, fun and contributing to society more highly than their male peers. They rated financial security and success less.

Most of the women interviewed had started their own businesses because they were interested in them, or because they thought they would be fun or allow them control over their own lives. None mentioned making pots of money as a motivation. Most were already comfortably off, as their partner was working.

Indeed, women millionaires work fewer hours than their male

counterparts – almost 10 hours a week less and they commute less too. (However, surprise, surprise, they do a lot more household chores and spend more time with the family!) They are also more likely to switch off on holiday. Nearly 80% of women forget about work entirely on holiday – as compared to only half of men.

Women are less motivated by money as a benchmark of success

Interestingly, women millionaires seem to come from more comfortable backgrounds than their male counterparts. This may be because the combination of being poor and female may be a handicap to women, but also because there is a tendency towards early motherhood in poor areas that may prevent women getting that first vital step on the success ladder.

Of course, women enjoy the money as much as their male counterparts: the spacious, beautifully fitted-out homes and second homes, the cars and school fees for the children – but their priorities are rather different.

Like male millionaires, wealthy women also like to save and invest and go on good holidays. However, they are far more concerned about school fees, charitable donations and having household help

female millionaires' youthful ambitions

1 To be part of a happy family
2 To do work which is enjoyable
3 To be financially secure
4 To be seen as successful
5 To contribute to society
6 To have lots of fun

learn from the millionaires

When Julie Hester, a straight-talking red-head, first started work cleaning at the mill her father owned, she could hardly have imagined that she would end up the owner of a thriving company, living in a glorious five-bedroom home, with a BMW convertible and able to holiday at the best hotels.

However, Julie's experience in the police force meant that she was already well accustomed to a male-dominated world when she started in business, something she feels has helped her succeed.

She also has huge stamina. Looking after four children and running a growing business is a near 24-hour job. The situation eased slightly when her husband Gary joined the business. But they were still sharing one computer from the living room, so they moved to a bigger house, using the garage as an office and employing their first member of staff. 'We were running up and down the country like headless chickens, doing searches,' Julie recalled. 'We knew that we could do with people in other areas to do the searches, but we weren't sure how to do it.'

Franchising provided the solution, leaving them free to concentrate on their local area. However, Julie admits that growth has been so rapid that it's 'been a little surreal'. However, she is insistent that she feels no different than five years ago. She still shops in the high street, only buying designer clothes if they are in a factory outlet and looks out for two-for-one offers in the supermarket. She is careful to put plenty of money aside for savings and investments because she says, darkly, 'you never know what could happen …' For Julie, the biggest advantage of having money is simply that she no longer has to worry about it.

female spending priorities

1   Savings and investments
2   Quality holidays
3   School fees
4   Hobbies
5   Charity donations
6   Good food and wine
7   Household staff
8   Going to the theatre, opera and other cultural events
9   Eating out at good restaurants
10 Top-of-the-range cars

than their male counterparts. They also rate a top-of-the-range car far less than men!

Children figure much more tangibly in the businesswoman's view, if she has them. While many senior men and male entrepreneurs are devoted dads, the needs of the children do not dictate their way of working. The same isn't true of those female entrepreneurs with young fami-

Female entrepreneurs often try to find ways to save time

lies. While most see their success as being beneficial to their children, over half believe that children can be spoilt by a parent's success. This may be why leading a 'normal' life is often very important to them.

Many female entrepreneurs also try to find ways to give themselves more time. Julie Hester, for instance, started The Property Search Group from her living room thinking it would be a part-time job and her first real premises was a converted garage at the family home. Mandy Haberman worked long hours – but was based at home.

One theory as to why there are so few successful female entrepreneurs is that the peak years when people start their own business (the

20s and 30s) coincide with child-bearing and rearing years, meaning fewer women have the time, or even energy, to get a business going. Priscilla Carluccio, for instance, had a hugely successful career as a photographer but gave up work when her second child was born, eventually becoming a *marchande ambulante*. (This is a French technical term for someone who buys and sells from markets. Priscilla was then living in France and started off selling pine furniture.) As the children grew older, so did the scope of her ambitions – becoming buying director of the Conran Shop, before marrying her second husband Antonio Carluccio and starting a business together.

Female entrepreneurs and directors who are married or cohabiting (and these are by far the majority) also need to rely on their partner's support which may, or sometimes may not, be forthcoming. Certainly those teams which seem to work best are either those where the husband works in the business as well or where he is already established as a success in his own area.

According to the Tulip survey successful women also have different strengths from the male. They may be more risk-averse, but they are also more likely to see themselves as good with people, practical and details-orientated. Priscilla Carluccio, for instance, believes that women bring an extra dimension to a company in being more maternal. 'We tend to be less competitive, more willing to negotiate. It's important for me that we have companies that are good for people to work in.'

There are other, subtle pressures on women too. In a largely male peer group, looks and presentation are very important. The women millionaires in the Tulip survey spent an average of £1,380 on their clothes with a quarter favouring designer wear, far higher than their male counterparts. They were also more likely to see their own attractiveness as being integral to their success. In their largely male-dominated world, women need every weapon they can get to fight their corner.

learn from the millionaires

For Sarah Tremellen, a vivacious, energetic woman, leading a normal life is hugely important, even though her own company turnover is now £15 million – but maybe that's because Sarah's product is supremely down-to-earth. Sarah spotted the huge opportunity of supplying bras to women with larger breasts, when she herself was pregnant and her bosom had expanded with her waistline. As she trekked from shop to shop in search of a supportive bra, she found that each outlet had only one or two in stock, 'And they were both hideous! I really objected to the fact that I had so little choice and the attitude was – very much – take it or leave it.'

She started Bravissimo, along with a partner, from her living room, looking after her baby by day, working in the evenings. But she says that it never felt like a slog. 'It was more like an indulgence.'

As the company grew, she found she had to deal with a whole range of issues from distribution and management, to retailing. However, she believes that one reason the business has been so successful is that she and her team have relied on their own judgement and common sense. 'Learning by having a go,' as she puts it.

In many ways, Sarah is a typical female entrepreneur. She started her own business because she wanted to be in control, rather than because she wanted to earn a mint. 'I loved the idea of creating something, setting it up, shaping it and developing it,' she says.

Like most female entrepreneurs, she did not take huge risks. Indeed, she points out that the risks were minimal, since her husband had a good job, and they were not dependent on her income. She and her partner each invested in £3,000 of their own money, so they were not beholden to the bank.

For Sarah, the support of her husband has been hugely important and he now works in the company alongside her. She feels, however, it is very important to have balance and time for her family in her life. Indeed, she recalls that when she first started, her son used to bring in biscuits as she packed up the lingerie.

Her attitude towards spending is also typical. 'I wasn't the sort of person who felt short of money before,' she says. 'I don't wear designer clothes, don't drive a flash car and I'm on the parent-teacher association at school.' For her, retaining a feeling of normality and sustaining her family life is hugely important. But she adds, 'It is hard to switch off and stop, because this is the business I love and it's part of my life.'

growing it

getting to multimillionaire status

'Investing is simple, but not easy.'
WARREN BUFFETT INTERVIEW ON CNBC w/MARIA

Up and down the country, there are millions of small businesses, from newsagents, to garden centres and beauty salons. Most of the small business people who run them will have that one business for their working life. These microbusinesses, nicknamed 'mom-and-pop-stores' form the mainstay of many families. However, few of these small business people will join a small mobile phone retailer and grow it into 170 stores within five years as Chris Gorman did. So how do you turn a successful small business into a much larger successful business?

goal-setting

For many entrepreneurs, the crucial difference between those who grow and those who don't is simply the scope of the goal they set

137

themselves. Those interviewed always envisaged themselves as success-ful and, to them, that success didn't mean rising to the heights of store manager, or running a one-off coffee bar. Once they had established the business, most had further goals to pursue.

According to Professor Elizabeth Chell, Director of the Institute for Entrepreneurship at Southampton University, the ambitions the owner has for the business are a crucial part of whether that business grows or not. Intention, coupled with vision and hunger, is the way she puts it.

If you like a quiet life and are earning a decent living then you may simply choose not to put yourself through the sheer hassle of finding new stores or markets, more finance or funding, and managing staff, to name just a few aspects. Then there's the increased risk of increased finance, increased overheads and the sheer costs of building a business and reputation. If you are already making a good living, you might well think that it's simply not worth the risk, hassle or nail-biting factor. You would be in the majority.

However, what differentiates those who want to grow a business, from those who will ultimately be millionaires, is they see growth, and the stress involved, as a challenge, a buzz. They are natural risk-takers and feel the risks are worth taking. For their restless nature, sitting still just isn't an option.

Intention coupled with vision and growth is the key to expansion

Sahar Hashemi did not set out to run one coffee store. She set out to build a chain of coffee stores that would provide a certain type of experience, a branding of the experience of coffee drinking. Karan Bilimoria also wanted to build Cobra as a brand. It is often the willingness to build a brand, in the retail area at least, that marks out the small players from those who will grow into larger ones. Antonio and Priscilla Carluccio are unusual in that Antonio had an established reputation both as a cookery writer and broadcaster, so that people already had certain positive associations with Carluccio's when they

138

opened their eponymous caffé. However, generally you have to start from scratch and that means thinking – long before it happens – about what your unique selling point will be and how you will build your brand. Having a blueprint for success is a vital ingredient in making sure it happens.

It is also true that for many small businesses if you do not grow, you eventually stagnate and then fall. Competitors arrive, your customers look for novelty, or a better price. In business, nothing stays the same and even to remain on an even keel takes hard work.

Indeed, many of the millionaires interviewed felt that if you didn't keep pushing for success, there was no plateau, just decline. T. Harv Eker, the business guru, summed up his philosophy: 'If you are not growing you are automatically dying.' In other words you have to keep challenging yourself. Even if you have a small business and do not want to grow it, you should be on the lookout for ways to grow within the business, new ranges, new services, more flexibility and so on.

learning to let go

Ironically, while you may have spent a great deal of time climbing up the career ladder or building a business, one of the characteristics of truly successful people is a willingness to let go of certain aspects of the business to concentrate on doing what they do best. In the early days of a career or building a business, it may be necessary to do everything you are asked to do or have to do, from opening the post and mailing goods, to sweeping the floor. Indeed, one of the great advantages of graduate trainee schemes is that they generally give the chosen graduates a comprehensive understanding of all aspects of the business.

Nevertheless, while it is crucial to understand your whole business, no one can be fabulous at performing every single function. The great financial director may not make a fabulous marketing director, for instance, while the brilliant PR may be useless at logistics. Many entrepreneurs are so swept up by their own enthusiasm and energy that they may not realise that their staff doesn't naturally have the same enthusiasm or energy, particularly if they are not enjoying the same ample rewards, or have no stake in building up the business.

As the business expands, letting go becomes crucial. According to psychological research, one of the greatest hazards to an entrepreneur is over-identification with their business. Many business people find it difficult to let others in, even if those others are far more expert than they are. For them the business is almost like a baby, and like a parent they find it very difficult when that child goes to school and starts to have other influences in their life. However, as with any child, letting go is vital if the business or child is to develop. Often the savviest entrepreneurs work out which roles they need to delegate – and then make sure they find the right people to perform those roles.

It is crucial to understand all aspects of your business, but you cannot be equally proficient at performing them

David Quayle (B&Q, Ritz Videos) has avoided the temptation to do everything himself. He grew B&Q from one store in 1969 to 26 ten years later, by clever delegation and incentivisation of his staff. 'I like having new ideas, new challenges then – despite all those people who raise their eyebrows and say it can't be done – making it work. Once it works, I like to find people who can make the idea work and move on.'

knowing your strengths, knowing your weaknesses

The most successful business people, directors and professionals have a high degree of self-awareness. Take Chris Gorman, for instance. On the problem-solving day for the *Mind of a Millionaire* series he was asked to throw a ball through a net, choosing the distance from which he wanted to throw it. Generally entrepreneurs, being risk-takers, tend

learn from the millionaires

Julie Hester and her husband Gary found that expanding the Property Search Group soon meant whizzing up and down the country, often with a poor cost–ratio benefit. Life became increasingly frenetic especially as the couple also had four children under the age of seven!

They soon realised that doing long-distance searches just wasn't efficient, but weren't sure of the way forward. Then, at a wedding, a fellow guest remarked that they should contact him as soon as they'd launched the franchise. They instantly realised that this was the solution they'd been looking for. Within weeks, they were off to a major franchise exhibition in Birmingham and, liking what they saw, signed up. Now the company has over 100 franchises, leaving Julie and Gary free to concentrate on their local area, while still retaining national involvement.

to opt for throwing from further away. However, he decided that he wouldn't stand back and throw from the greater distances since he knew his throwing skills were limited. So what would he do if he had to enter a ball-throwing competition? 'Find someone who can

Successful people concentrate on what they do best

throw a ball far better than me and employ them,' he quipped. This retort was humorous, but it contained an essential truth. There is no point entering a competition you don't have a chance of winning. People with a millionaire mindset realise this and concentrate on the areas they do best, as soon as they are able to do so, finding others who are strong where they are weak to do the rest. Few entrepreneurs have fabulous people skills for instance, or love micromanagement. They get other people to do that for them.

Alexander Amosu admits he finds the technical side of running a business – the accountancy, the contracts, the personnel issues – by far the most difficult. Alexander sees himself very much as an ideas person. 'I'm someone who likes to have an idea, get it up and running, start the business and make it work.' However, he admits that he finds many of the day-to-day issues less exciting. He has resolved this dilemma by selling part of his business, keeping a stake, and going on to creating the next.

By doing the following exercise you will have a better idea of your own strengths and weaknesses, and whether you therefore might need to employ people with certain skills.

exercise: strengths and weaknesses

Think about these areas. Mark them with either an S (strong) or W (weak). This should help you decide where you need to employ or buy-in talent.

1 Are you a good leader?
2 Do you find it easy to mix with people?
3 Are you interested in listening to their opinions and acting on them?
4 How much do you feel you understand others' motives?
5 Are you strong on detailed planning and do you enjoy it?
6 Do you have great ideas?
7 How good are you at financial planning?
8 What is your attitude to being part of a team?

Remember, even the most adaptable millionaire will need to engage services such as accounting, legal advice and advertising. It is well worth hunting out the best you can afford.

finding the right people

In the early years you may have to fulfil every business role yourself; from marketing manager to office cleaner, delivery agent to book-keeper. However, as we have seen, once you expand, doing everything is no longer appropriate or profitable. Finding the right people is crucial to any organisation. Indeed, according to the Tulip survey, multimillionaires, i.e. those who had been mega-successful in business, were more likely to rate finding good people as a priority, than those who had made less. However, as many of the entrepreneurs I spoke to have pointed out, finding them at the outset of the business when you are the new boy in town is very difficult. Talented people prefer to stick with an established organisation which they can be sure will pay their wages and offer them career progression. It takes a great deal of faith to leap into bed with a new company.

'No matter how great an entrepreneur you are, unless you have the right people around you to challenge you and help you along the way, it's still not going to work.' CHRIS GORMAN

Interestingly, the multimillionaires surveyed in the Tulip survey were more likely to ascribe a large part of their success to employing the right people. This may be because they are aware of the importance of getting the right people, or perhaps because they run larger businesses where it is easier to attract high-calibre employees.

So how do you attract the right staff? Clearly pay and incentivisation is important, but motivating your staff is vital. Priscilla Carluccio gives a talk to all of the waitressing staff before the opening of any branch of Carluccio's, stressing the importance of their role and the fact that a pleasant waitress or waiter can lift the spirits of a customer who feels down or has had a bad day. Placing the staff at the centre of the organisation is, she believes, crucial to good morale.

However, this emphasis on the central role of her staff is backed up by two weeks of intensive training before any opening, so that there are no slip-ups on the opening night. After all, the first experience of any service environment – whether it's a restaurant or florist – is the experience that determines whether you will come back. In catering,

learn from the millionaires

For David Quayle, co-founder of B&Q, one of the most pressing expansion problems of the early days was finding warehouse-style sites on the edge of town (in 1970, shopping was generally high street-based).

Whenever he found a suitable site, refusal of planning permission often came quickly behind. Finally, he located a disused supermarket in Margate, but it soon became clear that it was too far from his Southampton base to manage effectively.

By chance, a respected former colleague asked him for a job. David told him straight that he didn't have a job – but he did have a site. 'I told him to check it out and if he liked it we'd meet that afternoon at 4 p.m. under the clock in Waterloo station.' The conversation took place at 9 a.m., and by 4 p.m., under the clock, a deal was being hammered out, setting up an associate company, B&Q Kent. Other area companies followed, eventually covering England.

In many ways, David's way of delegating was an early prototype of the franchising operations that became so popular in the early 1980s. The managing director of each region would find the site, run and staff the stores. The head office would organise buying, merchandising and accounts. To motivate them, the MDs were paid a very low basic salary – but a high percentage of the profit. 'I suppose it was mean,' David chuckles. 'But on the day B&Q floated we had some very happy MDs because five or six of them became millionaires!'

people are particularly unforgiving. Eat a bad meal at a new restaurant, and you may not ever give it another try.

how much can you take?

Growing a business takes an enormous stomach for both challenge and risk. You also need to be able to handle the stress – and the lean years when nothing goes right and everything seems to be against you.

'It's a weak person who can't ride the wave and get on with life without moaning about what's gone wrong.'
TOM HARTLEY SENIOR

Going for rapid growth is a high-risk strategy and you need to be very clear of your vision and what you want from the businesses. This takes focus, the ability to rise to a challenge – and nerves of steel. It also takes incisiveness. Chris Gorman turned around The Gadget Shop in under nine months. One of his first moves was to take the merchandise out of the glass cases it was placed in and allow the customer to self-select. Being able to look at things without having to ask permission increased the customer's enthusiasm and willingness to buy. It sounds a little thing, but it makes a big difference. Being able to focus on details like this, while taking the strain of the bigger picture – and the bigger risk – is vital if you want to grow fast and to become truly rich.

to sell or not to sell?

How do you know you have really made it in business? When serious buyers want to buy you out. But the decision to sell is an intensely personal one. For some entrepreneurs, particularly theme entrepreneurs, they are so strongly involved in the business that they are unlikely ever to sell out.

Basil Newby, for instance, says he has had several offers to either

145

franchise or adapt his Funny Girls concept. He hasn't felt that any of the offers he has received have been right and so has kept the concept as it is, rather than risk it becoming something he wouldn't recognise.

Others – particularly serial and revenge entrepreneurs – will sell, as long as the timing is right. But how do you know when that is? The answer is you need to sell when things are going really well. All businesses grow, peak, plateau and fall off, as the market changes or something newer comes along, or competition increases. But deciding when to sell is incredibly individual.

- Ideally, you want to sell when there is still some growth in the market, and buyers are willing to pay a good price. Only the very luckiest sell at the peak and many, many people hold on to their businesses, hoping to hit that peak only to find that the peak has passed them by and they are rolling down the hill at an ever-gathering pace. Often these are people who were greedy, looking for an ever-higher price.

- Keeping an eye on the market is, of course, vital. You need to have a good idea, not just of how your company is performing, but of how the economy, your competitors and your market generally is doing.

- You also need to know your business extremely well. The finances, the staffing, the forward orders, the outgoings, any looming problems, where you feel the business will go (if you don't feel you've any new ideas, or can no longer manage it, it's time to think about leaving).

- Then it's a question of making it exciting to buyers. This is where your professional advisers, accountants, bankers and solicitors come in. Accountants have a range of perfectly legal tactics to present the business in the best light. It's the business equivalent of putting on the percolator and filling your home with fresh flowers when you are trying to sell it. You are not lying about the way you live, just presenting its best face.

🌐 Sometimes you may choose to sell the business outright, or keep a stake. However, it has to be said that if you do intend to sell, make sure you have plan B up your sleeve. While there is a tradition in Britain of selling up and retiring to do other things, if you are a restless person, with plenty of energy, you may find that boredom sets in as quickly as rigor mortis.

🌐 Another good reason to sell is simply that you feel you have taken the concept as far as you possibly can. Your motives may be far less financial than an eagerness to get on with the next idea, or doing what you know you are best at. While this type of sale is emotionally driven, you should still look to time it well to give yourself the maximum number of further opportunities.

other factors for success

Both Tom Hartley Senior and William Frame, who own a car and property business respectively, felt there was one crucial ingredient in their successful expansion – not being greedy. Greed can leave you with unsold goods. Tom Hartley, for instance, gives the example of a car that he had seen in a showroom and made an offer for. The salesmen refused to sell it on the grounds it was for retail sale. Three months later, the car was on sale at the price he'd offered – and still unsold. 'You won't go broke taking profit' is one of his favourite mottos and he points out that even through three recessions he has increased profit and turnover. William Frame, the Scottish property magnate agrees. He feels that it's vital in the property business not to be greedy.

Charging what the customer perceives as an acceptable price is important. Repeat business never comes from people who have been ripped off.

Similarly, it is important to remember that you need to have good relations not only with your employees, but with others who may be important to you. Priscilla

People will not come back if they feel cheated

Carluccio, for instance, has carefully nurtured relationships with her suppliers, taking into account their problems and expecting they will help her in return if she needs a sudden rushed order, or more products than expected.

growing your money

One way to make more money is to grow your business or, if you are a business person, to climb up the corporate ladder. But there are other ways that are equally important to millionaires. Indeed, for those 300 interviewed in the Tulip survey their number one priority was to have money for savings and investments.

There is a general perception that investing is an easy option, a risk-free gamble. In fact, done well, investing requires skill, acumen and research – with an element of luck thrown in. The 'average' millionaire spends over seven hours a week researching and monitoring his investments. This is over half the time that most of us spend watching TV! It is also a far greater proportion of time than most people spend on their investments – which is why those with a millionaire mind tend to invest more successfully.

Given that millionaires already have loads of money, and are careful into the bargain with it, why on earth do they do it? The simple answer is that money isn't a commodity that stays still. You are either increasing your wealth, or you are losing your wealth. If you have a million pounds now, and do nothing over the next year except spend, say £30,000, you will have £970,000 next year – but this will be worth even less than the year when you started with a million as you will have to allow for inflation. This is a similar process to the way a car depreciates. On the other hand, if you have a million pounds, invest some of it wisely, and spend £30,000, you may end up with a million the second year, or even more. While most people think of investments as stocks and shares, you also need to remember that, for the rich, there is a greater range of investment opportunities from property (often a good earner), to arts and antiques.

It is frighteningly easy to spend, spend, spend. Top sportspeople, for instance, can earn millions of pounds at the top – but their career length is limited. Some use the money they earn to allow them to either change career direction or invest it wisely. Others end up broke, having blown every penny.

In order to use your success to obtain the lifestyle you desire, you need to use money wisely. That means budgeting carefully, staying out of debt and understanding the principles of savings and investments. Once you reach a certain level of savings and investments, your money can work for you enabling you to reach new goals and diversify if you so choose.

So how do you set about launching a financial strategy that will grow your money, alongside your career goals?

First, you need to know what is going on in the financial and business world. Read the business pages and be prepared to take the time to become financially literate. In this sense, the web is a real blessing, allowing you to study company accounts and gain background information with comparative ease. For beginners two of the easiest and most enlightening reads on understanding financial matters are Alvin Hall's two books *Winning with Shares* and *Your Money or Your Life*. Here, however, are some very basic tips:

- You cannot afford to invest anything until you have cleared your debts (bar your mortgage).

- Ensure you have 3-6 months' salary stored in a high-interest bank or building society account. This is rainy day money, your fall-back fund in case of redundancy, an unexpected emergency, such as eldercare or added childcare costs, sickness or other problems. Putting your money in a savings account is, by and large, risk-free. You won't have a large return on your money, but you will be able to have access to it easily and know that it is safe.

Investment is a riskier process. The value of all investments can, as the adverts say, go down as well as up. Many people have discovered this to their cost when the stock market falls. For this reason, only invest money you could, if the worst came to the worst, afford to lose. Do not invest money that you need this month or next or for the mortgage. The good news is that although most investors have suffered losses over the last few years, historically the trend is for investments to go up over time.

Investing does not mean getting rich quick. You are unlikely to make an investment today and a killing tomorrow. You need to look at investment as a long-term strategy. Only invest money if you are prepared to keep it in the investment for around three to five years. If it is clear that you should sell it beforehand, great. However, don't make an investment that you may need to realise within the next year, or you could be forced to sell at a much lower price than you wanted.

It is important to know what you are investing for. Is it just for the pleasure of seeing your money grow? Or is it in order to afford a large house, a child's school fees or retirement? If you are investing for, say, school fees, you should opt for a less risky investment than someone who is investing for fun.

If you are near retirement and are looking to maximise your possible income, you will probably choose a less risky investment than someone hoping for a good, quick profit. Knowing what you want to achieve from your investments will help you decide how much risk you want to take – important in deciding where to put your money.

🟢 The classic lower-risk investment is investing in government bonds (gilts). Essentially, a bond means that you are lending that sum of money to either the government or a company. In return for your 'advance' they will pay you back the sum, with a contractual amount of interest at pre-arranged dates. The risk is that the institution or government may not be able to pay you back at the end of the agreed period. However, corporate bond-holders are paid out before shareholders which is why they are a less risky investment than shares, but a higher risk than a savings account.

🟢 A share, also known as a stock or equity, is a stake in a company, so that each shareholder is, in fact, a part-owner of the business. (However, it is only those who have sizeable amounts of shares, such as institutions, who will have any real say over company direction. You can, however, give your views at the annual general meeting and attempt to hold directors and managers to account then.) If the company does well your shares should go up in value so you can sell them at a profit or hold on to them in the hope they will go up further. If the company does badly or falls out of favour, your shares may well end up worth less than you paid for them. You can also make money when the company issues a dividend (the company pays some of its profits to shareholders). Shares may do very well when the company or market in general is doing well, but they can also fail spectacularly. The trick is buying and selling the right share at the right price at the right time.

🟢 You can invest in separate companies, cherry picking those whom you think will do well, or you may decide to buy into a unit trust – a portfolio of stocks and bonds – managed by a professional team. An ISA (Independent Savings Account) can be a tax-free way of investing a certain amount of money in a unit trust or in specific companies. However, the fact that the investment is tax-free does not mean that the individual ISA is any less risky than investing in individual stocks and shares. You should look carefully at what an ISA is investing in before you decide to invest.

£ When choosing what to invest in it's best to avoid having all your eggs in one basket. If you have your entire investment in 'No Chance & Co' and they do badly, you are in financial trouble. There is no sure-fire way of making good your return, particularly when markets are volatile, as they have been in the last couple of years and when there is an economic slowdown. However, some professional advisers suggest having just over half your investment in shares (including ISAs and unit trusts), around a third in bonds and 10% in areas in which you can access the cash quickly. Others recommend that you put 100% minus your age into shares. That means that as you get older and are starting to look towards your pension nest egg, your investments will become safer and more conservative. Other investments to look at include property for rental or sale and collectables.

£ Don't leave it all to professionals. Ultimately, it is your money, not theirs. Do take advice from an independent financial adviser, but then research what they say. Do the unit trusts or shares they suggest look like a good bet to you? How much money did these investments make for their clients last year? Over a five-year period? Look up companies on the internet and see how their shares have done historically. If a share has done badly, followed by doing even worse, what miracle do they have in the pipeline to restore it? Find out who the management are. Do they have a track record of success, or have they come from ailing companies? What did they do before coming to this company? How well did their previous company do before they arrived, when they were there and afterwards? (It is surprising how many people get appointed with a track record that is far from enticing when looked at in detail. Some, for instance, have a habit of leaving just before their chickens come home to roost.) Alvin Hall, the financial guru, suggests that buying a share without knowing its history is like jumping off a bridge without a bungee cord!

£ It pays to know what you are doing, so if there's a sector that you know a considerable amount about, then invest in that. Philip Green, owner of BHS, Burton, Dorothy Perkins, Miss Selfridge and Top Shop, has a wealth of understanding of the retail market – which is why he says that he does not have a penny invested outside it.

lifestyles

how the rich live and spend

*'With money in your pocket, you are wise
and you are handsome and you sing well, too.'*

YIDDISH PROVERB

Mr Jones lives in a village in the commuter belt in an unremarkable four-bedroom house with a spacious and neatly trimmed garden, lovingly tended by his wife. He wears Marks & Spencer shirts, many of which are five years old, and ties his wife bought for him from a bargain rail at BHS. He jostles into work with the commuter crowds in the morning, while his wife uses the family car, a five-year-old Ford, which he must get around to replacing, as soon as he has the time.

This morning, on the train, he looks at a couple of spreadsheets. He is working out how much income they've made from the three-bedroom villa they bought in the South of France a couple of years ago. His wife decorated it herself and he feels she has made it look stunning. It's a great place to tour from, too. He only gets there for a fortnight in August, but his wife is there every holiday with the children. One of the odd things about private schools, he thinks, is that they have much longer holidays than the village school down the road. More money for less teaching. Someone must be making a good profit. He hopes their education is worth it. He left school at 16 himself and it didn't do him any harm. Nowadays they seem to stay on until they are 93!

He notes that takings at the villa are up in the summer months. In general, he prefers to rent the villa out to some of his small social circle, but he's toying with the idea of advertising it more widely off-season. He finishes his calculations, gets out the mobile phone, simultaneously dialling while scanning the business pages. To the other commuters on the train, he doesn't look particularly rich. They'd place him as a middle-grade civil servant. In fact, he's a millionaire businessman.

Mr Brown lives in a spacious, six-bedroom, grade-two listed Victorian rectory at the other end of the village. The garden is still spacious even though he built an indoor swimming pool last year and an extra garage to house the Ferrari. (It was hell to get planning permission, though.) His wife employed an interior designer for the swimming pool, but didn't like the scheme and redid the décor herself, placing miniature trees around the edge and some of her (seemingly endless) collection of china plates on the wall. She collects plates and since, quite frankly, some of his senior team have wives who'll spend £2,000 on a dress, he's quite happy to indulge her. At least she still shops on the high street. She's booking a holiday this morning. The kids wanted to go to the beach, of course, but he can't sit on a lounger for longer than five minutes, so they've settled on a villa close to Pompeii. He always finds historic sites fascinating. Doesn't even think of business when he's exploring ruins, which is most unusual. It will be good for the kids' education, too. He has no regrets about sending them to the local village school, but he does feel that giving them a taste of European life gives them an edge.

He doesn't take the train. What's the point when you have a gleaming, new, top-of-the range Mercedes to take you in purring air-conditioned comfort? His wife has a four-wheel drive and, of course, there's the Ferrari which gave him such a buzz when he first bought it and saw the envy on the faces of his neighbours as he shot through the village. Brown's done well for himself, they say grudgingly. Must be a millionaire by now. And indeed he is.

He must take the Ferrari for a spin, perhaps when he's finished the round of golf he's promised himself at the exclusive club he joined last year. He's only had time for a couple of games recently. Good games, though: he won every time. But he must use it more often or it really won't be value for money.

The real millionaire is on average over 40, married with children and spends most of his waking hours working

Both Mr Jones and Mr Brown are self-made millionaires, but they have entirely different spending priorities. Indeed, in interviews with millionaires, it became clear that individually their spending priorities were as different as their personalities and businesses. Often the only common links were that they had vast, impressive houses (this was a major priority), several foreign holidays a year and were eager investors. Indeed, the Tulip survey shows that, in general, having money for saving and investments is the number one priority of both millionaires and multimillionaires, men and women, company executives, professionals and business people.

Millionaires are very different from their tabloid stereotype. The 'tabloid' millionaire is a single man in his 30s who spends most of his time clubbing or gliding up and down the Med on a yacht the size of a blue whale, surrounded by a brace of beauty queens like anorexic partridges hanging off each arm. The *real* millionaire is, on average, over 40, married with children, spends most of his waking hours working and relaxes by going on holiday or playing golf. Most live highly conventional, well-padded lives.

There are also huge differentials within the millionaire category. Not all millionaires are equal. In fact, two-thirds of all millionaires have less than £2 million in assets (though this hardly makes them eligible for a government grant) while the top 10%, (15,000 in number) average £6.5 million. Even at this level money does, it seems, buy happiness. Fifty-five per cent of the ultrarich (£3 million plus in assets) declare themselves to be very happy with their lifestyle, compared to just 43% of the poorer millionaires. The ultrarich are also more self-satisfied, seeing themselves as very successful, compared to 48% (less than half) of the poorer millionaires. This may seem odd when you consider that being a millionaire is, in our society, considered a badge of success, whether you are rich or ultrarich. However, the fact is that millionaires tend to meet other millionaires or look up to other millionaires and to judge their success by those standards, rather than, say, by average income, which has become largely meaningless to them. This means that those who have less are likely to compare themselves unfavourably to those who have more, just as, further down the scale, the man who has a studio flat may compare himself unfavourably with his brother who has a house.

Millionaires tend to judge their success by the standard of other millionaires

spending and saving

The millionaires profiled in this book are, by definition, extremely wealthy people, with wealth ranging from several millions to several hundred millions. None of them are beset by the money worries that afflict most people: bills, wanting a new car or outfit but being unable to afford it, credit card debt or worries about interest rates going up.

Nevertheless, that doesn't mean they are careless with money. Far from it. They haggle over purchases whether it's hotel rooms or cars, they only buy what they consider good value and are very careful over little things.

how do your spending priorities match those of a millionaire?

Do you think like a millionaire when it comes to spending? Would you use your money like they do? Take our quiz and find out.

Put the following in order of priority (1–10). It is important to have money for:

1   Charitable donations
2   Eating out at good restaurants
3   Fine drink and wine
4   Enjoyable holidays
5   Financial planning i.e. money for investment and saving
6   Hobbies
7   Household staff such as nannies, cleaners and gardeners
8   Quality cars
9   Sport, either club fees or watching it
10 School fees

(Solutions on page 182)

John Madejski, for instance, who has an estimated worth of over £260 million and a collection of Ferraris, Bentleys and other achingly expensive cars, confesses that he always turns the lights out after leaving a room.

In some ways they are extremely frugal

The simple fact is that people who value money don't waste it – and equally don't like to be ripped off. Just because you can afford expensive furnishings and boutique hotels, doesn't mean you want to pay over the odds for them. Efficiency, including budgetary efficiency, is often a component part of getting to the top. Indeed, those ultra-successful

how does your spending match up to a millionaire's?

1 How much do you spend on average on a meal for two with your partner?

2 Which of the following dishes would you rather eat in a restaurant: lamb, beef, monkfish, curry, fish and chips or a vegetarian option?

3 How much do you spend on the weekly supermarket shop?

4 How much would you expect to spend on a night out with friends?

5 How much would you expect to spend on giving a party for friends?

6 How much do you spend on holidays annually?

(Solutions on page 181)

entrepreneurs who own yachts, helicopters and second homes rarely leave them standing empty 50 weeks of the year. They are more likely to rent them out and make a tidy profit on the side. Ironically, the richer the person, the more likely they are to say it is vital to have money to invest.

Indeed, financially successful people are extremely good at looking at their possessions as assets, which may be one reason why they spend heavily on their homes, but extremely sparsely on their wardrobes. ('What's the point of having a load of depreciating assets hung up there?' one millionaire remarked.) Around half claim to spend less than £500 a year on their clothing, including accessories, shoes, underwear and ties (that's less than

Some confessed cheerily to having clothing that was over ten years old

£60 a month). Some confessed cheerily to having clothing that was over ten years old. Not surprisingly, given this budget, the average millionaire is not a frequenter of designer stores, preferring to buy cheap and cheerful clothes from Marks & Spencer, BHS (owned by Philip Green, the patron saint of entrepreneurs) or Gap. Six per cent, particularly those who had an unhappy childhood, even confessed to having their old clothes patched up.

'To me making money was freedom and success. I thought that when I made money I'd grow my hair long. But the sad thing is you become more respectable because you have your status and credibility to think about. I no longer feel like having long hair and dirty fingernails.' JOHN MADEJSKI

To some extent, this lack of interest in clothes is a gender issue. Most millionaires are male and many men simply aren't that interested in clothes. (One in five admitted that their wives did their clothes shopping.) Female millionaires tended to spend more, although they also preferred high street stores to designer boutiques. So it seems that if you want to emulate the truly wealthy, don't pop into Moschino – take a trip to Marks & Spencer!

home sweet home

While millionaires are far more careful with their money than the average person, when it comes to what they do choose to spend their money on, their priorities vary widely. For most of them, the purchase that most encapsulates their success is their home. Chris Gorman visited show homes he aspired to, in order to help motivate him to earn enough to buy one. Julie Hester feels that the most important purchase she has made has been her new home, a five-bedroom rectory. Basil Newby says that one of his childhood ambitions was to have a beautiful, big home in the country – which he has realised.

Whether it's a listed building or an ultra-modern house, a millionaire's home really is his castle or, at least, stately period house.

US research suggests that many millionaires are under-mortgaged. The 'average' millionaire in the Tulip survey lives in a four-bedroom, detached home with two bathrooms, worth £685,000, out in the countryside or in a village. (Though, according to Tulip research, those from a poor background and the ultrarich were more likely to have a town pad as well as more bedrooms.)

The average millionaire lives in a four-bedroom, detached home

So why are millionaires under-mortgaged? Probably because most millionaires would have bought their homes when they were growing the business, rather than when the business was at its peak. Moving home takes considerable effort and since the millionaire's home is comfortable, spacious and functional, once they've found one they feel happy with, many decide moving is not worth the effort. This may also explain why, despite their high income, only a third own a second home in Britain or abroad. Too much hassle and, for the poorer millionaires, a drain on income.

Cars are the ultimate status symbol for the multimillionaire

Cars also feature heavily in the millionaire or, at least, the multimillionaire, lifestyle. Nearly two-thirds of the ultrarich own a Mercedes or BMW, while a quarter own a Rolls-Royce or Bentley, the ultimate in status symbol cars. Of course, few multimillionaires content themselves with just one car. Drive up their imposing gravelled carriage drives and you are likely to see a four-wheel drive and possibly a Ferrari or Porsche as well. For the ultra-rich, flash cars symbolise both the financial security and success that they craved as children. Single millionaires, on the other hand, favour a Ford or Peugeot, with the ubiquitous Mercedes or BMW in second place. Like the ultrarich, their second car is most likely to be a four-wheel drive (great for driving around the grounds in winter).

on holiday

Millionaires work hard – but they play hard too. Almost two-thirds of them have three or more holidays a year, with 20% managing to take time off at least six times. The richer you are, the more often you go on holiday and the more you spend.

So what do millionaires like to do when they are on one of their many trips abroad? By and large they are not sun-worshippers. Several of those I interviewed expressed their impatience with sitting on a beach for more than a few days, or even hours. For them the inactivity soon sent them climbing up the walls and desperate to return to the adrenaline-filled world of business. This is, perhaps, a reflection of their enormous energy. Restlessness and sunbathing is not an easy combination. Indeed, the number one choice, according to the Tulip survey, is visiting historic sites, probably since this encompasses lots of walking around. Younger success stories are likely to enjoy activity/sporting holidays as well, pursuing victory in tennis or sailing with the same vigour they pursue success in business.

Restlessness and sunbathing don't make a great combination

They are not great fans of roughing it. You don't work hard to huddle round the calor gas stove in a leaking tent in the freezing rain. They love their deluxe villas and, for the ultrarich, five-star hotels, complete with room service, health spa and marble atriums.

'I could sit on a beach and chill out for the rest of my life. But I don't want to. When you've had the excitement of being on the roundabout and step off you want to get back on damn quick.' JOHN MADEJSKI

However, the richer the millionaire the more likely they are to work on holiday with entrepreneurs being twice as likely to keep on working as professionals, chief executives and other managers. Indeed, a third of entrepreneurs keep in touch with their business while on holiday, as opposed to a quarter of those working for companies or partnerships. Under half of entrepreneurs can completely switch off as opposed to nearly two-thirds of those who work for companies. Ultimately, when the company is yours the buck stops with you.

leisure and pleasure

Imagine you're a millionaire. How would you love to spend an evening? Dancing at an exclusive nightclub? Throwing a party at a top-notch restaurant? Or eating a roast beef dinner with your spouse? If the third is your favourite, then you already have an insight into the millionaire lifestyle. Millionaires are busy people so a relaxing night in with their wife comes way ahead of a night at the opera, dinner with friends or a rock concert.

However, despite their long working weeks, most are able to find time for their hobbies, largely because they prioritise ruthlessly and are not diverted by others' priorities. Tom Hartley Junior and Senior, for instance, both enjoy a game of golf, but their competitive natures ensure they play only to the highest standard, winning the pro-am at the Belfry, the Midlands' most prestigious golf club.

'I eat in the best restaurants, but I also enjoy eating fish and chips with my hands and sometimes that can be better than meals that cost three or four hundred pounds.'
TOM HARTLEY SENIOR

Golf features prominently on the millionaire agenda as does taking part in or watching sport. This may be because most are extremely competitive. On the other hand, many have unusual passions too.

Horses often feature in a wealthy lifestyle. John Madejski used to own horses, but found them too time-consuming, while David Gold owns several racehorses. Indeed, the 'season' and Royal Ascot, in particular, feature high on the millionaire

learn from the millionaires

a tale of two lifestyles

Robert Braithwaite, Entrepreneur of the Year, says that while he wants to earn a sensible amount of money, he is not overtly interested in money for its own sake.

Indeed, although he loves boats, the only Sunseeker he has owned was secondhand, because he felt he couldn't afford a new one. His current craft is a small Cornish crabber, the equivalent of a mini in the boating world. Robert takes pride that his major passion, apart from boating, is tramping across Dartmoor – and enjoying the odd pint or three after a good hike is very inexpensive. 'The things I love best don't cost much,' he says.

John Madejski, the serial entrepreneur and founder of *AutoTrader*, has all the trappings of an opulent lifestyle.

He has the dauntingly immaculate home (though he is currently trying to get planning permission to build a new home nearby). Then there's the car collection that includes Bentleys, Jaguars, Rolls-Royce and Ferraris (including one mounted like an exhibit in his private gym), exquisite art, the swimming pool, tennis court, private gym and, at one time, horses which grazed in his grounds. He even owns Reading Football Club, which he bought in 1990, not so much because he's an out-and-out football fan, but because he was the only local willing to take it on. Despite the hefty costs, and building a stadium, he is convinced he will make a profit on it. 'I'm going to make it work and take a profit out of it,' he says with passion. 'That will be my prize.'

He admits that he's become used to high living, eating out at top restaurants every day. Yet, he's also surprisingly matter-of-fact about this cornucopia of consumption. 'We are born with nothing and we leave with nothing. I also find it fascinating that once you can afford anything you desire, you find that you don't want anything.'

social scene, perhaps because these are costly, exclusive events that are also great for networking.

the limits of wealth

Ultimately, you can only eat three meals a day, drive one car at a time and sleep in one bedroom. So what do you do once you have literally too much money to spend? Tom Hartley Senior, for instance, admits he has made so much money that if he never worked for the rest of his life, he still couldn't spend it all: 'Which is a comfort zone to be in.'

Several of the multimillionaires featured in this book are big charity donors, from Karan Bilimoria, who supports a plethora of causes, to John Madejski, who finances the building of galleries and lecture theatres. (Though the Tulip survey suggests that for male millionaires, in general, charity-giving isn't a top priority. It is much higher up the list for women.)

If you earn, say, £13,000 a year, you might find it difficult to imagine how anyone can spend well over that amount on holidays. Indeed, when they were starting out, most of the successful people in this book would not have dreamed of doing so either. But what tends to happen is that expenditure gradually increases with income, so that a standard *'Rich' is someone who has 20% more than you do* of living which a millionaire might have coveted ten years ago, comes to be accepted as normal, even humdrum. 'Rich' is often, as we have said earlier, someone who has 20% more than you do.

Most self-made millionaires also become wealthy gradually, which affects their spending priorities. If you win the lottery, you can be earning £4 an hour one day, and worth £4 million the next, a huge psychological shift. However, if you run a business, or climb the corporate or professional ladder, wealth comes gradually, with an emphasis on continual upgrading, rather than going out and splurging. So, for instance, if you used to go to a one-star hotel in Italy, you may gradually decide to go to a three-star and then five-star instead. If you liked parties before you were rich, you will like them just as much afterwards – except that you will give more lavish ones. Money does not change your personality or interests, it just gives you more choices as to how you pursue those interests and more means to do so.

Naturally, once you have enjoyed the benefits of money, you become used to them. Certainly, several of the millionaires profiled, ironically often the richer ones, expressed the fear that they might lose what they had worked so hard to gain. Money liberates, but it also makes it much harder to go back to doing without. Once you've had a taste of the good life you dread going backwards which, in itself, can be a spur to earning more.

how childhood affects spending priorities

While all millionaires tended to be penny-wise, there were significant differences between those who had had unhappy or poor childhoods and those who had grown up in happier, or wealthier homes.

The Tulip survey found that millionaires who felt they had had an unhappy or poor childhood were, by and large, richer than those who had had happy or perfect childhoods – and were significantly more driven. They were far more likely to work on holiday than those with a more comfortable childhood. Not surprisingly their number one ambition as a child had been to have financial security.

While those from difficult backgrounds tended to be wealthier, they also were likely to be bigger spenders. They have more holidays (which they work through), and spend more cash pursuing their hobbies, eating out, and on expensive cars and antiques. For millionaires who had a challenging time as children, money is both security and a commodity to be enjoyed to the hilt, perhaps to compensate for earlier times. However, despite their lavish lifestyles, these millionaires are still less happy than those who had a good (but not perfect) childhood,

learn from the millionaires

Wealth not only brings material wealth, it brings status as well. You can party with the stars at a charity ball, or hire the biggest of big names to entertain your guests at your own bash. You can buy a football or rugby club or even get to meet the Queen.

John Madejski, for instance, amongst his family photos, has both an invite from the Queen and a picture of him meeting her.

David Gold says that one of the joys of owning a racehorse is that he gets to see the Queen at the winners' enclosure at Ascot. 'That's stunning for a boy out of the East End of London. The last time I saw her was in Canning Town just after the war and I just got a glimpse of her as her chauffeur-driven car went through the East End. I saw her for about ten seconds. And to be standing literally two yards away from her in the winners' enclosure is an excitement.'

suggesting that even the highest degree of success cannot give the security and contentment that a happy childhood fosters.

It seems that if you have been poor, you are well aware just how much happiness money can buy. As the first in their family to 'make it', the poor-boy millionaires are determined to enjoy all the things they had to do without – and to enjoy them in style. No wonder they tend to be both more competitive and bigger risk-takers than those with richer childhoods. Without the backing of a wealthy family, they know that it's entirely down to them how well they do. For them the stakes are so much higher.

friends – who needs them?

Millionaires love networking and meeting people who could be useful to them, or finding an opportunity to promote the business further.

where to meet a millionaire

When it comes to making money it helps to know the right people. So whether you want to meet a millionaire to persuade them to invest in your business, sell them life assurance or even marry one, here are a few tips:

- Do go South. You are much more likely to meet a millionaire in the South East or in Greater London, where nearly a third of millionaires live, than in the North (4%), North West (8%), Scotland (4%) or the North East (6%). After London and the South East, the Midlands are your best bet (14%), followed by the South West (11%).
- Don't move to Ulster and Wales. Only 2% of millionaires live here.
- Do join the golf club. Millionaires love their golf.
- Don't go down the pub. Only 6% of millionaires like to spend an evening there. If you are dining out, choose a traditional English or French restaurant over ethnic cuisine. (They much prefer roast beef to curry.) But beware, the ones you are likely to meet in a restaurant are probably already with their partner.
- Do take a tour of historic sites such as Pompeii or the Colosseum, preferably while staying in a five-star hotel.
- Don't crash out on the beach. Only 10% of millionaires can lie still long enough to get a tan.
- Do go to art galleries or the races; both seem to be a major passion for those with a cultured bent.
- Don't bother with a three-hour concert with the mobile switched off. Sheer hell for most millionaires.
- Do go to Marks & Spencer, BHS, or other middle-of-the road chains. How will you be able to tell who's a millionaire from who's not? Stand by the till. The millionaire is the one trying to haggle for buying a job lot!

But when it comes to superficial friendships, they are much less inter-ested, particularly the entrepreneurs who have a small circle of close friends, often unconnected with their business.

This self-reliance is reflected in the low priority they give to having a night out with friends, which rates far below a dinner out with their partner and, for the ultrarich, well below a night out at the theatre or opera. They would also spend considerably less on a night out with friends than with their partner.

However, the millionaires who are successful corporate players or professionals are both more sociable and place a higher value on having a wide circle of friends and colleagues. This is because those who opt for climbing the company ladder tend to be people who are both team players, able to fit into a regulated environment and have emotional awareness. Professionals and managers would spend consid-erably more on a party for friends and family than would business people – probably because they'd invite more people.

the millionaire marriage

In general, millionaires are not only married or co-habiting, they are more likely to be happily married to their first wife than the general population. Three-quarters of millionaires are married or co-habiting, with a similar proportion having been with their partner for over ten years. It seems that when it comes to success, having a stable relation-ship counts. Indeed the millionaires themselves acknowledge their debt to their partners. Three-quarters of company directors and two-thirds of entrepreneurs believe their wife has played a large part in their success. (Corporate spouses may be viewed as more helpful either because they are expected to take part in company functions or client entertaining, or simply because executives are, in general, better team players and more likely to acknowledge the contribution of their wife as part of that team.)

Interestingly, only a third of the ultrarich believe they have been very successful in their personal lives, compared with half of the poorer millionaires. This is probably because, by and large, the ultrarich actually work longer and harder than the average millionaire, leaving them less time to spend at home with their family. While the millionaire divorce rate is way below average, the ultrarich are twice as likely to have been divorced as the other millionaires, their drive meaning they spend longer at work and devote less time to their personal lives. Even at these income levels, work–life balance is still a major issue.

A stable relationship is important for success

It is no revelation that in general being successful in your working life correlates highly with success in your personal life. If you enjoy your work, are successful at it and fulfilled, then your levels of anger and frustration are likely to be lower than those who are miserable in their jobs, at a low level and on a low income. The amorous effect of cash, as W.H. Auden termed it, has been acknowledged as far back as Jane Austen, when Elizabeth Bennett in *Pride and Prejudice* decides she likes Mr Darcy a whole lot more once she has viewed Pemberley, his stately home.

Money can also shore up those relationships which are basically strong, but which are also vulnerable to outside pressures. There is an old Yiddish saying that when money flies out the window, love flies out the door. The well-off family can employ babysitters to give them time together, can buy faster medical treatment and care if a family member is ill, and can relax through holidays and hobbies. The impoverished family cannot pay for support or afford many pleasures. Love on the dole is hard work. (Interestingly, 95% of lottery winners are also married to the same person as before their win, suggesting that an increase of cash, however obtained, can actually solidify a partnership.)

However, this does not entirely explain the success of millionaires' marriages. After all, most of the millionaires interviewed for this book had met and married their wives before they were wealthy. In the early days many wealthy people – and their partners – had to take considerable risks to establish themselves, particularly if they were entrepreneurs. Their home may have been put up as security, income reinvested in the business, and there are few entrepreneurs who have not experienced tough times or outward failure.

mr multimillionaire v mr millionaire

While both millionaires and multimillionaires are wealthy, there are big income differences between the two and big spending differences as well.

- One in five millionaires are female – but only 2% of multimillionaires.
- Multimillionaires were hugely ambitious even as young people. They wanted to be both financially secure and seen as successful.
- They work harder – 64 hours on average as compared to 55 for poorer millionaires. But they also employ more staff to ease their domestic life.
- They are more likely to run their own business than work for a company. They are also more likely to see themselves as enthusiastic and impulsive, than poorer millionaires.
- They are better at recruiting good teams than single millionaires and place more emphasis on finding the right people to work for them.
- They spend more and place a higher value on status symbols such as cars, eating out at top restaurants and owning a second (or third) home.
- They see themselves as more successful in their work life than 'average' millionaires, but as less successful in their personal lives. They are also more likely to be divorced.

As we have previously seen, millionaires are almost to a man (and woman) stickers, rather than quitters. They also trust their own judgement implicitly. Both these qualities mean that they are more likely to persevere with a marriage rather than bail out at the first squall. What's more, both partners seem to share the same aims: financial security backed up by hard work.

There are other factors too. Building a high-flying career or new business is a major investment both in terms of time and money. You cannot be working your hardest on a new deal, new business, or building a reputation, if you are also bedhopping at a rate of knots. If you are serious about building wealth, you won't have a lot of time in the early days for acting the playboy.

Millionaires tend to work at their marriages

Divorce is an enormously expensive business. If you think of financial security as a game of snakes and ladders, divorce is always a very long snake. (The average divorce costs £13,000, so for those on far-from-average incomes, the costs will be proportionally higher.) If you are a borderline millionaire, a divorce will ensure that you never quite make it financially while you will also have to spend huge amounts of time, energy and heartache dividing assets, allocating childcare and arguing over who is entitled to what. A divorce generally involves two houses, the division of assets, and maintenance for both spouse and children. This is a heavy burden for anyone who is in the development stages of a career or business. If you are vaguely discontented in your marriage, but need more income, you would be well advised to try working on your marriage as a first step to avoid financial crisis.

the millionaire wife

This may sound a sexist sub-head, but the simple fact is that four out of five millionaires are men so their partners are likely to be either female or same-sex if they are gay.

In the US, there are courses gold-digging women can attend on how to find a millionaire to marry. While marrying a millionaire may sound attractive – access to wealth, status, jewellery and designer clothes – you actually pay a hefty price for your material rewards. Given the actual job description beforehand, many women would be happy to turn the post down.

In the US there are even courses on how to marry a millionaire

The wife of a millionaire will probably marry her husband well before he is wealthy and she will get to enjoy – and endure – the roller-coaster years of establishing the business, or climbing the corporate ladder alongside him. This may involve backing her husband, even when no one else does. Chris Gorman, for instance, admits that many people felt he was mad when he decided to leave a secure job for what was then a very small business. His wife Mary, however, backed him all the way. She believed in him and supported him even in the days when he was working over 80 hours a week and yet making little headway.

There are also three people in the marriage of any very successful person: the person, the spouse and the business or career. Often the career is far more demanding than the relationship. One stoic millionaire's wife confessed that she sometimes felt she came fourth in her husband's priorities. She felt the business, the computer and his mobile took first, second and third places!

A top job, whether as an entrepreneur, executive or professional, can often require 12 hours a day, six days a week commitment – with the seventh spent either recovering or thinking about the next batch of work. Then there's the business travel, the calls at weekends and the cancelled holidays when something comes up. Even when successful people aren't working, they are often thinking about their work.

learn from the millionaires

Richard Prout, dotcom entrepreneur, founder of SmartGroups.com and now of Gliant.com, admits that his first marriage foundered partially on the long hours he worked.

His wife would phone at 5.30 p.m. to ask when he'd be home and he'd say an hour later, meaning a whole lot later than that. Then she'd phone repeatedly, becoming increasingly worried. 'Now if I'm away for two days Jenny just thinks I'm busy – though she'd expect me to be polite when I got home. She's my best friend.'

Tom Hartley Senior, who owns a top luxury car dealership with his son Tom, has been happily married for over 20 years and has four children. He works hugely hard, but feels that having his dealership situated in the grounds of his home has allowed him to combine work and family life since long before working from home was fashionable.

Even from a very young age, his children have had their own little seat in his office. There they have been able to be with him, watch what he does and chat when he's not busy. Not a single client has objected. Tom feels many have appreciated the family atmosphere and it has helped them realise they are dealing with an established business. He feels that he has had both 'success in marriage and success in business. I'm around my wife and children all the time because my business unit and home unit are so close together. I have the perfect life, and if I never did anything else from tomorrow, I have lived my dream.'

the right stuff

According to Thomas Stanley in his book of US millionaires, *The Millionaire Mind*, millionaires are, in general, as shrewd in their choice of a wife as in their business dealings. According to his survey, millionaires were actually less likely to rate physical attractiveness as the most important quality in a wife, than non-millionaires. Far from the traditional image of the millionaire with the stunning trophy wife, most stated that other qualities were as important as physical attractiveness. These included honesty, cheerfulness and unselfishness. When it came to what initially attracted them, intelligence, sincerity and a happy nature scored highly.

While research gives no indication that British millionaires choose any different criteria than their fellow men, the wives of millionaires are, in general, not only highly devoted to their spouses and in sympathy with their aims, they are also extremely capable in their own right. This is because the wife of a self-made millionaire will probably shoulder virtually all of the responsibility for the household herself. It will be her job to look after the children, visit their schools, to get the car fixed or the roof repaired, the dining room redecorated and arrange the children's dental apppointments. While most millionaires are doting fathers and try to spend time with their children, this is quality time and play time rather than the basics of packing the lunch boxes or organising whose turn it is to come over to play.

Millionaires are often doting fathers, but would rather spend quality time with their children than sorting out the nitty gritty of their lives

Indeed, the fact that British millionaires employ so little help seems to imply that their wives are, by and large, not in employment (it's hardly as if they need the money).

While the stereotype of the millionaire is of a man surrounded by a retinue of staff, from butlers and chauffeurs to personal shoppers, this is far from the truth. Indeed, by far the most common help is a cleaner. (The Tulip survey showed that around half of millionaires employed a cleaner; two-thirds of millionaires with young families and multimillionaires were more likely to employ a cleaner.) Gardeners were also popular (most millionaires live in villages or suburbs rather than in the city, and have large plots of land). However, only 20% of those with young children had a nanny – and other help such as chauffeurs, caterers, personal shoppers and designers were very much for the ultrarich. Rather than a huge retinue of staff, the modern millionaire tends to have a highly self-sufficient and capable wife, who organises the family's entire domestic life. This is a major undertaking and her partner appreciates her for this. Several millionaires spoke admiringly of how their wives managed the home front, so they had 'no hassle' when they came home.

The modern millionaire has an independent and accomplished wife

The high value that millionaires place on their wives is also demonstrated by the fact that they spend a considerably higher amount on them than on other friends and family. The average millionaire spends £400 on his wife's birthday present, rising to £800 for the ultrarich. Many millionaires selected dinner with their wife as their favourite night out (only 1% opted for dinner with an attractive colleague), rather than an evening out with friends or a cultural event – perhaps because they have so little time together.

It is also helpful for the partner of a millionaire to have plenty of common sense, to be laid-back and to lack egotism. The partner of a successful person, male or female, is often in their shadow, the spare hand at corporate functions, with a title of 'the wife of ...', rather than status in her own right. It takes both unselfishness and devotion to accept that.

Most millionaire marriages are based on a breadwinner husband and non-earning wife. However, while these marriages are very traditional, it has to be remembered that most millionaires are in their 40s

learn from the millionaires

Antonio and Priscilla Carluccio are high flyers in their own right. Antonio is a successful restaurateur and broadcaster. Priscilla has been a photographer, director and stylist, and trend forecaster. Antonio, now 66, and Priscilla co-founded the Neal Street Food shop 12 years ago and Carluccio's Caffé five years ago.

Although they work together they both have very different skills. Antonio is 'the mouth of the business' according to Priscilla. He creates the menus, works with the chef and is the company spokesperson. Priscilla does the marketing, development of sites and product development. 'From a business point of view it's a fantastic partnership,' says Priscilla. 'But in a personal sense, it has to be controlled.'

She admits that they both have strong views and do conflict, on occasion. However, they manage the potential for argument both by negotiation and having different areas of expertise. Priscilla acknowledges Antonio's expertise when it comes to food. He admires her business brain. 'I'm spontaneous. She is more calculating – and she is generally right.'

Although the Carluccios have differing areas of expertise, they are united when it comes to the core values of the business. Both are passionate about small producers, about producing quality food and both are eager to create a family business atmosphere as they expand. Early on they were, for instance, offered the opportunity to open 20 of the caffés in the US simultaneously, but decided against it on the grounds that they would not be able to exercise the same control as they are doing over their openings here.

This sort of unity over the actual vision of the business, and the direction they want it to take, is vital. It is easy for a family business to come unstuck if the parties have different visions. However, the Carluccios have a clear focus and defined areas of responsibility that solve many of the potential problems of husband-wife teams.

and 50s. Younger millionaires are more likely to have wives who either have their own career, possibly part-time, or who actively work in the business alongside them.

Interestingly, while most of the millionaires interviewed were in long-term relationships or marriages, the Tulip survey also threw some light on who was most likely to get married. Risk-takers, for instance, are both more likely to get married (after all marriage is a risk) and to stick with their spouses, since they trust their own judgement. The Tulip research also found that the millionaires who were introverts were far less likely to get married, suggesting that shyness is a block whatever your wealth or position.

husband to a millionaire wife

If being the wife of a millionaire male requires special qualities, being the husband of a millionaire woman requires even more. While marriages where the man is the main breadwinner are highly tradi-tional, women entrepreneurs tend to have 'new men' who are not only involved in their business at a senior level, but are perfectly willing to cook and muck in on the domestic side. Julie Hester, for instance, whose husband Gary is her finance director, recalls how they have always shared domestic tasks since her days as a policewoman and says her husband's input and support has been vital in establishing the business. Some of the most successful partnerships are those where both partners are involved in the business, but with separate and non-conflicting roles.

So what do these statistics mean for the aspirant millionaire? If you are single, they suggest not only that you should think about the priority you want to place on your personal life, but about the selection of your partner. While chemistry is always going to be a key ingredient, it's also important to find a partner who shares your values and is willing to support you in them.

learn from the millionaires

A football or rugby club is the ultimate rich man's toy. Multimillionaires and billionaires (including one lottery winner who bought his local team, Hastings) buy them to enjoy and a couple have even paid to get themselves five minutes on the pitch.

David Gold co-owns Birmingham City Football Club, the culmination of a long passion for football. He remembers as a boy being taken to a Birmingham City match. The crowd, the spectacle and the sheer excitement enchanted the boy from a poor East End home.

He was also a talented footballer himself and was almost signed professionally for West Ham. However, his father refused to sign the release papers, condemning him to continue his apprenticeship as a bricklayer, an occupation he hated. David admits that at the time he was distraught. But his passion for football never left him and today he feels that, 'Although I'm disappointed I didn't achieve every boy's dream to become a professional footballer, I've had the best of everything because subsequently I've become a director of a football club and many people dream of achieving that.' For David Gold, his purchase of Birmingham City represents the ultimate success of his life over tremendous odds and he is passionately devoted to it. So far, he, his brother Ralph and David Sullivan, who is co-owner of the club, have spent £17 million on it, a decision he feels is both 'foolhardy and brave'.

Solutions to quiz (page 160)

1. A millionaire expects to spend £40 a head on dinner for two with his partner.

2. Their favourite dish is roast beef or lamb, followed by the more rarefied sea bass or lobster. Less than 10% would opt for a curry or Chinese meal and only 1% are vegetarians.

3. A third of millionaires claim to spend a staggering under-£60 a week on the supermarket shop. However, the mean average figure is £90. Those under 45 were likely to be the biggest spenders. So if you spot a man or woman buying up two for one items, they are as likely to be a millionaire as on a tight budget. Millionaires love a bargain just as much as, if not more than, the rest of us. However, it may also be that they dine out more than average and so need to spend less in the supermarket.

4. Nearly two-thirds of millionaires would expect to spend under £100 on a night out with friends. However, the average works out at £145 a night, bumped up by the small number of multimillionaires who would spend over £1,000.

5. Millionaires tend to have a small circle of friends, which is perhaps why a third would expect to spend less than £100 on their nearest and dearest. However, the mean score is £668, with just under a half opting for between £100 and £500. So if you are planning a party, go gentle on the Twiglets and guest list if you want to emulate millionaire spending priorities.

6. Millionaires love their luxury holidays. The average millionaire spends £6,700 rising to £13,700 for the multimillionaires. The average spend is just under £10,000 a year. Holidaying regularly – even if they work through them – is part of the millionaire mindset.

Solutions to quiz (page 159)

The number one priority for millionaires is to have cash for savings and investments. This is followed by having sufficient money for great holidays. Third comes money to indulge in hobbies. Fourth on the list comes money for school fees, followed by fine drink and wine. In sixth place is quality cars, followed seventh by money for sport (taking part in or watching). Eighth comes money for paying for staff, followed by charity donations, with eating out at good restaurants coming in at number ten.

executive success!

how to make money as a corporate player

'You cannot motivate the best people with money. Money is just a way to keep score. The best people in any field are motivated by passion.'

ERIC S. RAYMOND

Becoming an entrepreneur or self-employed is not for everyone. If you have been reading the preceding chapters, and their tales of roller coaster risk-taking and complete absorption in the business, with a mixture of horror and awe, then starting and building a major business is not for you. What's more, if Dr Atkinson's questionnaire on page 77 suggested a strong affinity with corporate values this is most likely where you will flourish best.

Corporate high achievers are different. If you like the stimulation of a large organisation, work best as part of a team, pride yourself on your excellent communication and political skills, then you will probably want to utilise those skills within a company setting. Corporate achievers and, indeed, those working in administration and the public service, do have a slightly different outlook on life. The Tulip survey revealed that those working in companies or the public service tend to have larger social circles, enjoy socialising more and also find it easier to switch off from work.

Success is easier to come by if you are doing something you are good at and enjoy

However, this sociability and detachment from work comes with a price tag attached. In the main, business people are wealthier than company types (who are in turn wealthier than those working in the public sector). Corporate millionaires average a mere £2.3 million as opposed to £3.1 million for the entrepreneurs. However, don't feel too despairing if you are a team player: those at senior levels still earn very high salaries and enjoy expensive company cars and holidays. Indeed, the Tulip survey found that corporate players are actually more lavish when it comes to things such as throwing parties for friends.

Put simply, you'll still do very nicely, thank you, if you get to the top of a medium-sized or large organisation – and you are more likely to get to the top if your skills and values are best fitted to this approach.

Entrepreneurs have such a distinctive mindset that despite their huge business ability, many would find the confines of a large organisation unfulfilling and many would not succeed within one. Indeed, some entrepreneurs started their own business largely because they felt they were unemployable, or couldn't bear dancing to someone else's tune.

Entrepreneurs may not be suited to corporate life

Many highly successful chief executives and managing directors admire entrepreneurs – but few would want to become one.

how to maximise your income within a job

1 At interview never take the first salary offered. Try to negotiate a better one.

2 Look for jobs where performance is rewarded either through share options, bonuses, or other commissions. You want to show you can deliver.

3 Some companies set goals for employees. Meeting your targets can show your worth. However, in firms without goals or specific performance indicators, you will need to tell your boss about your brilliant performance and what you can deliver. Do not expect them to notice.

4 Do not be shy of asking for a pay rise. However good your performance, very few bosses will offer you one.

5 Prepare the case for your pay rise. Show what you have achieved, what you bring to the firm, what others in comparable firms are earning and so on. However, if you are going to ask for a pay rise, you need to show that you have already proved you are worth it.

6 Aim higher than you expect to get both in terms of salary and career progression.

7 If you feel you are under-valued and under-paid, look for another job. However, do not threaten to get another job unless you intend to carry out this threat.

8 Remember that salary is not the only indicator of income. Benefits such as private health care, pension contributions, travel expenses and so on should always be discussed and quantified.

So if you do want to climb the corporate ladder, here are some of the values and skills that will help you succeed. Remember, too, that while there is only one CEO or MD of a company, it is possible to be highly successful on the higher branches of the company tree. For instance, if you are passionate about marketing, you might start as a marketing assistant in a small company, move up to marketing manager there and then move to a larger company as marketing manager, eventually ending up as a marketing director for one of Britain's major PLCs. If you find it difficult to make decisions unilaterally, but enjoy implementing them, you may want to consciously avoid taking the top job, preferring to be a valued deputy. The important thing is to go as high as your talents, skills and will determine.

essential qualities for successful management

good managers show emotional intelligence

Emotional intelligence means just that – the ability not only to understand and empathise with people – but to use that understanding to motivate them.

In modern management, emotional intelligence is actually valued as highly as intelligence. Emotionally intelligent people are able to use people skills to a high level. They can get on with people within the organisation and outside as well. They can put themselves in the shoes of their juniors – and their seniors – and use that understanding to motivate the people around them. They are able to communicate well and give feedback.

Emotionally intelligent managers understand that if there are to be redundancies, it is better to come clean and explain what is happening and why, before the rumour mill gets to work.

Emotionally *unintelligent* managers award themselves a big fat pay rise two days after the redundancies.

Emotionally intelligent people are, not surprisingly, people-people. The Tulip survey revealed, for instance, that company players had bigger social circles than entrepreneurs and spent more on partying with them.

they are team players

Good managers are team players. Many of the most successful managers played team sports as youngsters. They understand the importance of teamwork and acknowledging the contribution of others. They are good listeners and delegators, something entrepreneurs often find difficult as their identity is so bound up with the business.

The Tulip survey of millionaires shows that corporate types are also far more sensitive to what other people think of them than entrepreneurs. Only a quarter said they were not affected by what others thought of them, as compared to half of those who owned their own business. They were more likely to see their main fault as over-conscientiousness than arrogance. Indeed, nearly half of company millionaires stress that they are good team players as well as results-orientated.

This dependence on other people is also shown in the company directors' beliefs about their own success. People working as top directors or in senior posts in the public service feel that luck has played a far greater role in their success than entrepreneurs do. They also place more emphasis on meeting the right people, as opposed to being self-reliant. In an organisation, whom you meet – and your relationship with them – is vital to your success. When you start your own business, your success is largely in your own hands.

company people follow company rules

Organisations are very like schools and colleges – the institutions most people move from in order to join organisations. They have their own rules, many of which make sense, a few of which don't, their own ethos and corporate culture. If you are a member of an organisation and you hope to achieve within that organisation, it is vital you buy into that culture and play largely by the rules.

As we have already seen, entrepreneurs are rule-breakers. This sort of short-cutting can make them very successful as business people, but it does not make for promotion or success in an organisation, where the process of how things are done may be as important as the results. Indeed, the Tulip survey found that few managers described themselves as 'enthusiastic and impulsive' compared to 40% of those who ran their own business. By contrast, managers saw their style as calm and relaxed. They are also less likely to view themselves as creative and more likely to see themselves as details-orientated.

company people are good at multi-tasking

As a successful company executive you need to be able to cope with doing several tasks and keeping in mind several priorities at one time. While you need to be single-minded about your ambitions, you will need to understand a multitude of different, competing priorities, from marketing to finance to personnel, and to be able to decide between those priorities. Is it more important, for instance, to implement a training programme at a particular time, than increase profits? How much of your budget should you give to marketing and is this marketing idea a runner in any case?

Professor Andrew Kakabadse, Professor of International Management at Cranfield School of Management, one of the country's leading business schools, has been involved in the Top Team Survey, a survey of over 12,000 top directors in 16 different countries.

top ten reasons why millionaire company directors believe they have been successful

1   Honesty and integrity
2   Enjoying work
3   Working hard
4   Able to get on with others
5   Intelligence
6   Being in the right place at the right time
7   Being self-disciplined and success-orientated
8   Good health
9   Taking opportunities
10 Being good at delegation

Interestingly, entrepreneurs place less emphasis on intelligence, luck and remaining healthy. They place more emphasis on taking opportunities. What's more, successful managers believe that meeting or employing the right people is more important than any personal qualities they may have. Managing people is, indeed, a people business.

He points out that many top executives had a period in their childhood where they had to overcome hardship. They often succeeded by planning and prioritising across several conflicting priorities. For instance, a child may have wanted to study hard at school, but owing to family circumstances, needed to bring in money too. By understanding and managing these conflicting demands well, they learnt the important skills of time management, prioritising and multi-tasking. Good chief executives need to juggle a whole host of priorities from business reputation and profit, to staff morale and public perception. They may be single-minded about the company and their own success, but they need to be several-track minded to create that success.

Of course, it is easy to specialise within a company, for instance in marketing or personnel. However, in order to make the most of your role, you need to understand the bigger picture and how the component parts fit.

they are details-orientated

Good managers are pragmatists and they are willing to sweat the small stuff as well as look at the bigger picture. They also tend to deal in the art of the possible, rather than tilting at what others think is impossible. Today many of the most successful companies are expert in cutting costs, achieving efficiencies and creating more streamlined structures. None of these are hugely creative processes. They require the detail and financial knowledge of an accountant, rather than the creativity of an artist. If you feel you are more creative than pragmatic, look for either a specialist role within an organisation or join a small or medium-sized one where your creativity can create business, as opposed to managing the existing product in a larger, more established one.

they are lucky

While only a few entrepreneurs acknowledge luck as being a major factor in their success, company directors and senior executives feel there is much more of an element of being the right person at the right time for the right company. It is easy, for instance, to describe the character traits that are likely to make someone successful in a company, but far harder to say which of the people who have those character traits will ultimately make it to the top job.

learn from the millionaires

Des Benjamin, a solid, intense man, has always considered himself a team player. While he swam competitively as a young man, he also loved rugby, the archetypal team sport.

When he came to HSA he found a team demoralised by Victorian working practices. He felt certain that if the culture changed, productivity would improve.

He feels that it is vitally important to understand the point of view of employees – the emotional intelligence that is imperative in organisational leadership. His first innovation was to start a company newsletter to improve communication. He then had to look at other ways to convince the staff that a change was on the cards. 'I had no credibility, no track record, no credentials. When I arrived I was seen as just another big-mouth, overpaid manager who would look after themselves and treat everyone else like serfs.'

Over time, he made a series of promises – and showed that he could deliver. He promised there would be restructuring without redundancies, and delivered. 'Over a three-year cycle people begin to trust you.'

The change in corporate culture has paid off. The team now gets through over 50% more project work than could be expected, staff turnover is down and income up.

Des feels that it is extremely important for senior executives to look beyond their own careers and to think about what they can bring to the organisation. 'I was once told by an MBA that on his first day in a new job, he started looking for his next job. I find that intensely self-serving.' However, he also adds that in order to bring value to the organisation, you need to believe in the organisation itself. Loyalty, in business as in marriage, is so much easier if you have a good relationship.

the right background

Top corporate managers and directors come from all sorts of back-grounds, rich and poor, happy and unhappy. Indeed, the Top Team Survey found that while there were chief executives who had been academic whiz-kids, there were also chief executives who had left school at 16. In all environments common sense can take you a long way, while in many, having a certain streetwise quality can be absolutely vital. For instance, in a hospital setting you might imag-ine that senior doctors would be better at running the hospital than former senior nurses. In fact, this is often not the case. This is because doctors are used to a degree of deference and to using nurses as a filtration system for dealing with complaining customers. Nurses, by contrast, are at the sharp end, having to deal with, and empathise with, members of the public, cleaners, doctors and a wider variety of hospital staff. Doctors can more easily alienate

Being streetwise is important

traits that make for success in a large organisation

- Vision
- Tenacity
- Self-belief
- Financial awareness
- Political awareness
- Hard work
- Dedication
- Communication skills
- Flexibility

vital staff such as cleaners, as they have not had dealings with them. Nurses, on the other hand, are more likely to understand their point of view and how they work.

Nevertheless, the increase in the number of students getting degrees and the increasing emphasis on qualifications means that anyone aspiring to rise up the corporate ladder would be very wise to get a qualification, in order to get off the starting blocks. Two-thirds of the directors of companies interviewed for the Tulip survey had attended university or college full-time. Over two-thirds had a professional qualification. It is therefore wise to get your degree – but Professor Kakabadse points out that you are equally wise to extend your knowledge of life and the world of work. In fact, working for a fast-food chain can be more educational than shadowing a high-flyer as you will learn the street-skills necessary for dealing with a wide range of people.

the right company for the right person

Picking a good company is vital to your success. According to the Top Team Survey 48% of the success of chief executives and other directors is down to personal qualities, such as drive, courage, tenacity and ability to communicate. However, 52% of success was down to choosing the right environment. Choose the wrong company and, however clear your vision, sharp your intelligence and brilliant your communication skills, you will either not do very well or may, indeed, be fired. So what makes a good company actually depends very much on your personality. A cut-and-thrust type may not thrive in a cosy, collegiate atmosphere. A team player will not enjoy a highly individualistic firm. You may not fit, for instance, if all the senior management come from the school of hard knocks while your background is Eton and The Guards.

Success is partially down to choosing the right company

Choosing the right context for yourself is highly important. While to outsiders there may be little to choose between, say, one telecoms company and another, or one law firm or another, the culture can be hugely different and that can make the difference as to whether you fit and thrive, or don't – and wilt.

For instance, in one culture it may be fine to talk openly about company difficulties to the press or staff. This might be seen as open management. In another culture such openness could be seen as making a bad situation worse, being a blabbermouth or even out and out disloyalty. One organisation may encourage team spirit, another may place emphasis on individual contributions.

So how do you find out which company is for you? To some extent, it is largely a matter of trial and error and very few successful people have managed to avoid at least one company they didn't feel comfortable with. However, as is often the case, research can help you avoid some mistakes. Find out as much as you can about any company you might want to work for. Ask people who work for the organisation too. Ideally, you want to work for a company where you respect and can learn from your boss, where you can advance your career on merit, rather than on marrying the boss's daughter, and where there is scope for training. All things being equal it is better to work for a company where the employees take pride in their place of employment and enjoy working at it, rather than one where they do not. However, it has to be said that at the outset of your career, you may not be inundated with offers and it could be very much a question of who picks you. Nevertheless, as you progress to more senior levels, picking the right environment matters more and more.

If your values don't chime with the organisation, start job-hunting

When you do make a move you need to quickly assess whether you believe in the organisation and like the way it is run, and whether you will be able to move up the ladder within it. A good analogy is that of family life. In a well-run family each member knows the others' strengths and weaknesses and can work with that. In one torn apart by squabbles, members are either intolerant of each other's weaknesses or jealous of the others' strengths. What may be highly acceptable in one family may be unacceptable in another – but both may be equally happy.

If you realise you don't fit, or your values don't chime with the organisation, you need to start looking for another job. However, do

exercise: are you and the company well-matched?

Ask yourself the following questions:

1 Do I recognise the critical issues in this company and my department? Do I believe I can play a role in solving them?

2 How is this company differentiated both externally and internally from its competitors? (To outsiders Pepsi and Coca-Cola may seem similar – but they may feel very different to their employees.)

3 How do I as an individual add value to this company?

4 How do I get on with my colleagues, my bosses? Is it a strain or do I understand where they are coming from?

5 How well do I understand my own character, motivation, drive? Do my character, motivation and drive find echoes in the commercial objectives of this organisation?

remember that while it might be wise to move once, moving repeatedly within a short period can be damaging.

In order to have a better idea of whether you and your company are well-matched, ask yourself the questions in the exercise on page 195. Working out the answers to these will help you in a huge variety of ways. It will help you to see how best to obtain answers that will suit the company and address its needs when you are presented with problems. It will help you work out how you fit in and also the best way to approach office politics.

moving up the ladder

You may find yourself in a position where you are a good middle manager, respected by your colleagues and earning a decent salary. Now you have to ask yourself if you really want to move up. What will the benefits be? What will the costs be?

Research on this issue is contradictory. Research for *The Sunday Times* shows that middle managers are the least happy in their jobs. On the other hand, the Top Team Survey shows that over a third of managers with seemingly high managerial skills fail to make the transition from middle to senior management and leave within the first year. This is often because they have not thought through the consequences of moving up the ladder: the fact that they will have to cope with increased pressure, visibility, complaints and responsibility.

Some managers find the transition to senior management too stressful to cope with

Many find the experience both stressful and damaging. They find the added responsibilities and decision-making higher than their stress threshold can cope with. For others, there is increasing conflict between home and family life as they have to work longer hours. It is therefore essential if you plan to move up the ladder that you know what you are taking on and you have your family's backing.

Professor Kakabadse feels that at the highest levels, the idea of work-life balance is risible, like expecting the Prime Minister to stop making decisions at 5 p.m. each night so he can care for little Leo. You need to love your work because, make no mistake, it will be your life. This may be one reason why there are still so few women board directors of top companies. They simply aren't prepared to sacrifice their family life to the extent required.

In order to find out what sort of role you really want to aim for, think about the following questions.

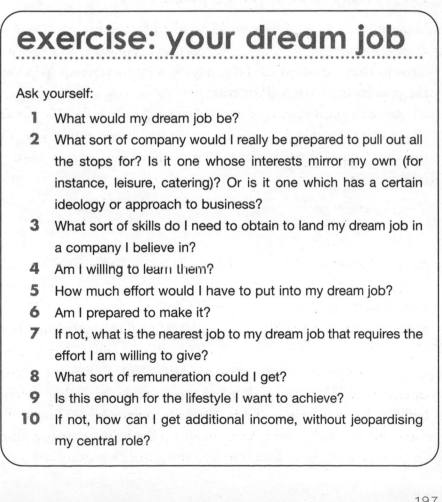

exercise: your dream job

Ask yourself:

1   What would my dream job be?
2   What sort of company would I really be prepared to pull out all the stops for? Is it one whose interests mirror my own (for instance, leisure, catering)? Or is it one which has a certain ideology or approach to business?
3   What sort of skills do I need to obtain to land my dream job in a company I believe in?
4   Am I willing to learn them?
5   How much effort would I have to put into my dream job?
6   Am I prepared to make it?
7   If not, what is the nearest job to my dream job that requires the effort I am willing to give?
8   What sort of remuneration could I get?
9   Is this enough for the lifestyle I want to achieve?
10 If not, how can I get additional income, without jeopardising my central role?

learn from the millionaires

Philip Williamson is now Chief Executive of the Nationwide Buillding Society, a respected and respectable job, but his first introduction to work was an unusual one. He spent a year as a volunteer on a Fijian island, Rotuma. It was so isolated that the arrival of the coconut boat once a month was a major event, and Philip frequently fished for his supper. He feels that year had an enormous impact on the way he managed others, giving him perspective on others' feelings and a healthy dose of humility.

Indeed, Philip stresses that although he is hugely competitive (he played sport to a high level in his youth) it is vital to pick the right field in which to compete. 'You need to think how can you add value to this business, rather than what can you take from it.' To do that you need to believe in the business itself. This is because at the top levels, the working week is intense. Philip leaves home at 5.30 a.m. on a Monday and until Friday night is focused on work, staying long hours and often taking part in evening events.

Philip knows at first hand how important it is to make sure your outlook and values match your company's. His one career detour was to a company where he simply didn't fit. He was in a senior position at Lloyds TSB but was offered the chance of promotion and a much higher salary by a smaller entrepreneurial firm. Flattered by the offer, he took it, but was soon unhappy. Although he got on with his colleagues, he discovered he simply didn't have the same mindset, approach and values as they did. After two years, he took a £50,000 drop in income to move to the Nationwide. 'I think there is a certain business chemistry that has to be right. It's the same as buying a house. You can buy a house that looks great, but after two years, you realise it just isn't the right house and you have to move on.'

For him Nationwide was the perfect fit and he moved swiftly up through the senior ranks from Marketing and Commercial Director to Retail Operations Director, giving him an overview of many aspects of the business. He feels this ability to understand and empathise with all aspects of the business is key. At the same time, he also points out that while managers have to deal with the bigger picture, 'You have to be close to the detail. That's why I spend one day a week out of the office whether it's at a branch or call centre.'

Like Des Benjamin, he also sees himself very much as a team player, although he admits he is happiest leading the team. Indeed, he says that the Nationwide's employee satisfaction rating has given him great pride. 'If people feel they are being rewarded fairly, treated fairly, if they enjoy work then they give that much more. It's business sense.'

For Philip having fun is crucial to his working life, whether it's taking part in a Nationwide fancy dress party dressed as a Bee Gee or hosting their annual charity ball.

Indeed, he believes that enjoyment of the job is more important than financial reward. 'It's great not having to worry about whether you can afford to go away for the weekend. But it isn't the money *per se* that counts.'

He believes that, ultimately, there is an element of luck as to whether you get to the top. To impress you need to be able to shine, but you need to get that opportunity to shine in the first place – and some of that is down to luck. However, he also believes that if your sole reason for wanting to climb the corporate ladder is the financial package, you probably won't make it to the top at all. 'You have to enjoy the business, believe in the business and ultimately give more to it than you get out.'

how company directors differ from entrepreneurs

- 💷 They see themselves more as team players and less as self-reliant.
- 💷 They believe time management is crucial.
- 💷 They go on holiday more – although they spend less on each holiday. When there they switch off from work.
- 💷 They are more likely to rate going to the opera or a classical concert as a favourite night out than entrepreneurs. They are also keener on dinner with friends and family and likely to spend more on them.
- 💷 They are more likely to live in a small village, or town. Entrepreneurs prefer a country estate.
- 💷 They are less likely to own a second home.
- 💷 They are more likely to own a Ford than a Mercedes.

8

passing it on

how to make your child rich

'The best career advice given to the young is,
"Find out what you like doing best and get
someone to pay you for doing it."'

KATHERINE WHITEHORN

You have now learnt the skills, values and qualities that matter when it comes to becoming a major success. You may well have wished you'd known all this earlier. However, if you have children you will have the chance to pass on much of what you have learnt. Interestingly, many of the millionaires had strong views about both what they thought children could learn from their experience and the impact of wealth itself on children.

Four in five questioned for the Tulip survey believe that the children of wealthy parents have a great start in life, with over half believing that success breeds success. However, they did acknowledge that wealth can bring problems such as children being spoilt, or less willing to work, or even just being too privileged. Most interviewed for this book were also concerned that their children should learn to manage their own money. 'They don't get it just because they ask for it,' was a common refrain. This makes sense. Successful people often have to practise deferred gratification and careful budgeting in the early years. This is often one of the reasons for their success.

Careful money management can help your child learn the same skills. There is a good chance that if your child sees you saving, budgeting wisely but still enjoying the odd indulgence and reward, they will learn that money is a commodity to be controlled and enjoyed. If they see you forever in your own personal boom-and-bust cycle, they may well emulate it later on, or rebel by becoming ultra-cautious and Scrooge-like.

It is odd that while there is huge emphasis in our society on teaching our children about sex, a child can get to the age of 18 without knowing how to budget, how to shop around or understand comparative pricing or APRs. *Basic money management means being able to budget*

So how can you promote a healthy attitude to money? The first thing is to understand what healthy money management means and to initiate it. According to Dr Pat Spungin, child psychologist and entrepreneur, basic money management means being able to budget, taking a long-term view of your money so that you save and understanding what things cost.

money talk

Start introducing your child to the concept of money at around the age of seven. (They study money in depth in year two in the national curriculum.) Before this children are too young to understand the concept properly and their grasp of mathematics will be too insecure for them to be able to handle it well.

One of the easiest ways to teach about money is to give pocket money. However, do not give this for the everyday chores your children are expected to perform. Doing chores is part of family teamwork and children shouldn't expect payment for routine obligations. At the same time it's fine to incentivise them to take on extra chores, for payment.

Other ways to encourage good money management amongst pre-teens include:

'My seven-year-old didn't believe I was a millionaire. He thought if I was I would drive a Ferrari and give him a new computer.'
JULIE HESTER

- Encourage your child to save for something they want. For younger children, it needs to be something they can obtain within a couple of weeks, as their patience and attention span is limited. They will soon realise that saving for things only increases the enjoyment of them. As they get used to saving and become more mature you can increase the length of time (and the value of the item) that they have to save for.

- Don't always give them toys on demand; let them learn to save for them or earn them.

- Giving your child a piggy bank to save in really does make it easier for them to accumulate their cash.

- Break their pocket money up, so that it's easier to save part of it. For instance, if you give £2, give it as two £1 coins, rather than as one, so that they can more easily decide to put £1 away and spend the other. Children find it easier to save for something if they can have a little to spend each week.

- Set 'saving' goals for them. For instance, if they want to save £10, give them a small reward or extra incentive when they reach the £5 milestone.

❸ At the supermarket show them how to use a shopping list and get them to compare prices, look out for two-for-one offers, etc. Don't be nagged into buying things that are not on the list. Encourage them to work out whether one item is cheaper than another (great for helping with their maths too) or how buying in bulk saves money.

❸ Start a bank account. Some banks give incentives for child savers such as lockable piggy banks or colouring-in books. However, hard interest should be a major factor in your decision.

❸ If they want something they don't need, such as designer trainers, come to an agreement whereby they will save a certain amount and you in return make up the rest. (The government uses this principle for certain projects, known as like-for-like, or matched, funding.) This helps them to distinguish between what they need and what they want. It also allows them to keep up with peer group pressure, while learning to handle money.

Let children learn by their mistakes – if they make a bad purchase once, they are less likely to make it again

❸ Let them learn by their mistakes. If they decide to save for something expensive, but it's poor value, tell them. If, however, they decide that's what they want, let them save for it, have it and endure the disappointment. It will teach them two valuable lessons – all that glitters is not gold, and if it seems too good to be true it normally is.

❸ If you are a single or weekend parent, don't give guilt offerings. Your children need your time rather than your presents.

❸ Don't give pocket money advances if they have spent it all. Otherwise, they may soon associate advances as a means of being bailed out and this may encourage them later on to get into debt.

teaching teens

An allowance is a great way to introduce teenagers to budgeting, understanding the value of money and living with the consequences of their own actions. However, do first of all make sure that both they – and you – understand what is to be included and what is not to be included. Will their mobile phone bill be included in the allowance? What about study aids? (You are probably overtly optimistic if you expect them to buy study aids or school books out of their own money. Remember if *you* want them to have it as opposed to them wanting to have it, you may need to pay for it.)

Throw the piggy bank out! Make sure they keep the bulk of their allowance in the bank or building society so they need to withdraw it, rather than have it always so temptingly to hand.

It is fine for children to want to fit in, but you should encourage them to think about why they want certain brands. Do they want a brand because they believe it is better quality, or because it will give them status with their peers? Will they still want the purchase in three months' time? This will help them think about their own motivation and assess their spending priorities. However, you do have to give them the freedom to make mistakes, buy clothing you don't like or items you feel are poor value.

Be tough. If they blow their money on a purchase they later regret or that's poor value, or they want something else later, do not bail them out. They will soon learn to make wiser choices.

Encourage your older child to take holiday or weekend jobs. Saturday jobs in shops, serving in cafés, babysitting or odd jobs are all a great start to the world of employment and will help them learn what the real world is like. Discourage them from quitting the job at the first problem.

● Start to discuss your finances with them. Show them the phone bills, supermarket bills, etc., so they understand the cost of living. Give them a notebook to record their outgoings and income.

● Encourage them to think about debt. It's easy to spend on a credit card, but all too easy to accumulate debt on it too. Make sure they understand that debt has to be paid back – with interest!

● Show them ways to shop smarter – discount stores, secondhand, bartering, rental, etc. Discuss the pros and cons.

● Don't constantly harp on about money, but don't make it a taboo subject either. It is vital your teenager understands the value of money but also that money should be a servant rather than a master. You may need a certain amount of money to obtain the lifestyle you want, but it is the lifestyle rather than the money that is the focal point. Encourage them to focus on their skills and ambitions rather than money as an end in itself.

helping your child succeed in life

Throughout this book you have read case studies of hugely successful people. While they are all different, they have certain values and aptitudes in common, a mindset that has led to their success. Many of the qualities they display – a willingness to work hard, energy, focus and ambition – can be nurtured in childhood. While your child has to make the decision as to what they do with their life, you can help influence their values and teach them skills that will help them succeed, whatever field they are in.

do you have a budding entrepreneur in the house?

Some of you will have read the tales of youthful entrepreneurs' salesmanship with surprise and admiration. Others will have spotted similar traits in your own child. If your child wants to run their own bring-and-buy sale or sell cakes to their schoolmates, don't discourage them. After all, no one has to buy their offerings. At the same time it helps to be aware that many schools discourage commercial activities, so it may be wise to do so off the premises. It's also important that you encourage your child to understand the value of fair trade – not ripping off their classmates left, right and centre. Most of the millionaires in this book say they succeeded through not being greedy, so it helps for your child to learn that lesson early on.

- Let a younger child help out at a car boot sale or school fête, so they can learn the principles of buying and selling.

- If your older child wants to start their own small venture, don't discourage them, but do make sure they have the financing in place and understand just how much they will need to earn to make a profit.

- Make sure they understand that starting your own business can be a positive career option.

- Many secondary schools run business challenges or enter teams for Young Entrepreneur of the Year. Find out if your child's school participates.

thinking focused

When they are very young, children naturally find it hard to focus. However, by the time they reach junior school, you can help them start to set short-term goals for themselves. These should be specific and achievable. There is no point expecting your child to be the best reader in the class by next term if he is dyslexic. They should also be goals they want to reach too, for instance if they want to improve on their spelling test, by trying to get one more spelling right, to learn to ride a bike or swim a width. As perseverance is important, encourage them to keep trying, if they don't succeed at first.

Once your child achieves a goal, do reward and praise them. Encourage them to set goals they can achieve for themselves so their confidence grows. Always remember to work with their personality. Setting a shy child the goal of enjoying a party, may be attempting to force the issue. If they want to attend a party as a goal, fine, but do remember they may not enjoy it. Give 'rewards' such as a treat or an outing for goals they achieve.

Encourage them to keep trying as perseverance counts

As your child grows older, the goals should become more complex and longer term. However, by the teens it is vital that your child wants to achieve these goals for *themselves*, rather than for you. Do encourage them and validate their goals, and encourage them to believe that they can achieve them. It is amazing how empowering that belief can be.

It is also important to allow your child to follow their own interests and aptitudes. Encouraging your child to become a doctor if they want to be an artist simply won't work. At this age if your child has no idea of their future direction in life (and most do not), it is better to simply encourage them to follow their interests and abilities. By the time they are ready to leave school, they may well need more specific help to find their direction.

Ultimately, what is important is that they feel satisfied with the area and direction they choose, and are able to do as well as they want to within it. There is nothing more frustrating than being stuck in a job you hate, with a career progression that seems pointless.

If your child isn't academic, it's essential that they find areas where they can succeed. Hobbies are very important, whether it's running, riding or rhythm and blues. If they find it hard to achieve academic goals, they can set goals in terms of their hobbies, personal development or other interests. Summer and weekend jobs are great for children of all abilities in expanding their experience and helping foster people and money skills.

Goal-setting will help your child achieve self-discipline and will encourage perseverance. This in itself is a major step towards success. It is amazing how many people lack follow-through or are daunted by the first hurdle. Children who have been taught to set goals and follow them through have a major advantage.

hard work counts

Self discipline is vital to success in life. We all know people who chop and change jobs as often as the rest of us change our underwear, or who can never finish any project no matter how small. You are doing your child no favours if you allow them to skip their homework, fail to do their chores or not complete tasks. It is not the actual work or even the quality that matters as much as learning to stick with something and follow it through.

However, to do our best, we all need *motivation*. Some people find it easy to motivate themselves, others need plenty of praise, rewards, regular feedback and support. Children are no different and it's important that you work out – and use – their motivational triggers. Some children take pride in work for its own sake, others need incentivisation. Whatever your child's motivation, you can really help by emphasising that it is the effort they put in that really matters.

helping your child overcome failure

Failure hurts. Yet all of us will fail at some time in our lives and most of us will fail fairly often. But how seriously that failure affects us depends very much on our perceptions of it. In primary school, a child might have imagined they'd win the egg and spoon race – only to lose it to a rival. They may not be selected for the school play or the choir, or they may fail to achieve their cycling proficiency certificate. As they grow older the failures become more difficult – failing to get into a certain school, or passing a certain exam, or crashing (hopefully not literally) out of the driving test. The fact is that failure is part of life and a child who has never failed has, in some ways, a rude shock coming to them later on. After all, even if you go on to win a Nobel prize, or set a world record, sooner or later someone will win two Nobel prizes or beat your record. Indeed, psychologists believe that parents who protect their child from ever failing are doing them a disservice, as it flies in the face of life.

Of course, there is no point setting your child up for certain disaster, for instance putting them in for the top violin exam when they started to play only three months ago. However, do not stop your child taking an exam or trying something out just because they might fail. Failure is part of learning and the earlier we experience it – and move on – the better we are at dealing with subsequent failures.

To some extent, it is not failure itself that matters, but our own attitude towards it. If every failure is a major deal and a child who has failed is punished (even if they tried very hard) for every failure, they soon learn to think of failure as something to fear. They will become willing only to try things where they are guaranteed success. On the other hand, if you accept their failure, commiserate, or encourage them to learn lessons from it and then move on, they not only learn what went wrong, but the failure isn't so terrible in itself. Indeed, some might argue that most of us learn more from our mistakes than from our successes!

However, while it is important not to make too big a deal of failure, it is important to learn not to make the same mistake twice. For instance, if your child failed their maths exam, you should work out why this happened. Was it because they didn't do any work? In which case they can easily work harder next time. Was it because they find maths very difficult? In which case, do they need more teaching or, if you can afford it, a private tutor? Are there certain areas which need work and others which don't? Or was it a technical mistake, like answering the wrong number of questions, that let them down? By helping your child analyse where they went wrong, you can help them put it right next time.

It is not failure itself, but how we deal with it, that determines our reaction to it

helping them deal with criticism

Everyone gets criticised at some point, but what you need to learn is how to distinguish positive criticism (criticism designed to help you) from negative criticism (criticism designed to wound you).

Positive, constructive criticism is designed to help a child improve. Positive criticism is normally couched in such a way that it lets a child know what areas they are struggling with, need to improve – and how they can do it. Positive criticism is worth listening to.

Negative criticism is hostile and unconstructive. Negative criticism is phrases such as 'you are really stupid', 'you are bad at maths', 'you can't do that', 'you'll never manage it'. Negative criticism saps morale, and makes us feel bad without suggesting a way out of the impasse. Highly successful business people are very good at seeing hostile criticism for what it is – and ignoring it!

my advice to a youngster

Alexander Amosu, founder of RnB Ringtones, now RnB World:
'You've got to make your own decisions and own choices in life. If you work hard and stick with it, things will happen in the end. If you've got determination and motivation no one can stop you. Sure, there are going to be projects you will try and fail, but keep working at it and one day it will happen, like it did for me.'

Robert Braithwaite, Managing Director of Sunseeker International, British boat builders:
'It's vital to have a vision of what you want to achieve and then set the goals to work towards that. Don't attempt to leapfrog your goals. Just go about achieving them step-by-step.'

William Frame, Director of Braemore Property Management:
'Work harder than everyone else and have plenty of enthusiasm for what you are doing.'

Chris Gorman of The Gadget Shop believes children are natural entrepreneurs:
'If a child falls off his bike, he gets up and gets on it again. If we waited until we were 25 to learn, we'd get on, fall off a couple of times and never bother again.'

Mandy Haberman, inventor of the Haberman Feeder and Anywayup Cup:
'In this country, teenagers are very much steered towards thinking of jobs in companies or professions. I think we need to make it clear that running your own business can be a very satisfying option and is one to consider.'

Tom Hartley Senior, founder of Tom Hartley, luxury car business:
'A penny saved is a penny earned. If you don't waste it, you won't want for it.'

John Madejski, founder of *AutoTrader* magazine, now running businesses ranging from hotels to publishers, 129th on *The Sunday Times* Rich List:
'Every individual brings something to the party: it's just a question of finding out what it is.'

David Quayle, co-founder of B&Q:
'Know all the knowable facts about the business before you go into it. For instance, my daughter came to me with an idea to run a teddy bear stall. So I asked how many teddy bears would she need to sell on a Saturday? What is the teddy bear market? If half of teddies are sold to newborns, what proportion of that market do you need? You need to know all the facts you can. And once you do know all the knowable facts, it's time to take a deep breath and do it.'

summary

Do you still want to be a millionaire? If so, hopefully the information and anecdotes in this book have given you loads of ideas and you already have a game plan. Many of the millionaires interviewed for this book like to outline the most important points or goals on paper, so they can refer back to them time and time again. Here are ten of the most important thing to remember when you start to work towards that very first million.

1 If you want to be a multimillionaire, be an entrepreneur. Owning your own business is where the really big money is.

2 Believe you can do it and you are halfway there.

3 You need to want it body and soul – and be prepared to put the effort in – especially in the early days.

Set goals for yourself in your career and personal life. Pick your priorities and stick with them.

 Drive and ambition are vital.

 Expect to fail at least once – learn from your mistakes and let them go.

 Don't play it by the book: learn to think laterally, do it differently.

 Take a chance – risk-taking is vital to success.

 Don't let others pull you down.

 Love what you do and you'll want to do more of it and will make more money from it.

Good luck!

further information

reading

Anyone Can Do It: Building Coffee Republic from our Kitchen Table, Sahar and Bobby Hashemi, Capstone, 2002

Sin to Win: Seven Deadly Steps to Success, Marc Lewis, Capstone, 2002

The Millionaire Mind, Thomas J. Stanley, Bantam, 2001

What Self-Made Millionaires Really Think, Do and Know: A Straight-talking Guide to Business Success and Personal Riches, Richard Dobbins & Barrie O. Pettman, Capstone, 1999

Winning With Shares, Alvin Hall, Hodder, 2002

Your Money or Your Life, Alvin Hall, Hodder, 2002

Lloyds TSB Small Business Guide by Sara Williams gives advice on starting a small business. Free to Lloyds business customers, or available via the website www.smallbusiness.co.uk or in many bookshops

organisations and information

Business Link is the national business advice centre. They can give a variety of information from starting up a business to accessing a wide range of business support organisations. There is a Business Support Directory to help you find if there are any low-cost loans or grants available for your business and the website can help you find your local Business link. www.business.link.org Tel: 0845 600 9006

Human Factors International is an innovative firm of corporate psychologists and business consultants. They help companies and individual entrepreneurs to identifty and develop potential at the individual, team and organisational levels. www.humanfactors.co.uk and www.peoplefactors.com

Human Factors International Ltd.
Edstone Hall, Stratford Road, Henley-in-Arden, West Midlands
Tel: 01926 843717 email: a.atkinson@humanfactors.co.uk

The Prince's Trust has a Business Programme offering low-interest loans, grants and mentors to 18-30-year-olds who want to start a business. www.princes-trust.org.uk Tel: 0800 842842

Shell LiveWIRE helps 16-30-year-olds start and develop their businesses and hosts a national competition, Young Entrepreneur of the Year. www.shell-livewire.org Tel: 0845 7573252

I very much hope that you have not only enjoyed this book but that you have found it useful. If this book does help you to 'Think Yourself Rich', we would like to hear your story. You may even be featured in a follow-up for Optomen Television. To let us know how it worked for you, write to: *Mind of a Millionaire* at Optomen Television, 1 Valentine Place, London, SE1 8QH.